QUALITATIVE DATA ANALYSIS
FOR EDUCATIONAL RESEARCH

Qualitative Data Analysis for Educational Research

A GUIDE TO USES OF SYSTEMIC NETWORKS

JOAN BLISS, MARTIN MONK, and JON OGBORN

with additional contributions from:
PAUL BLACK
HARRY ELLIOTT
JANET HOLLAND
NANCY JOHNSON
TONY ORGEE
D. MICHAEL WATTS

CROOM HELM
London • New York • Sydney

88/0010466

© 1983 J. Bliss, M. Monk and J. Ogborn
Croom Helm Ltd, Provident House, Burrell Row,
Beckenham, Kent, BR3 1AT

Croom Helm Australia, 44-50 Waterloo Road,
North Ryde, 2113, New South Wales

Reprinted 1987

Published in the USA by
Croom Helm
in association with Methuen, Inc.
29 West 35th Street
New York, NY 10001

British Library Cataloguing in Publication Data

Bliss, Joan
    Qualitative data analysis for educational
    researchers.
    1. Educational research
    I. Title II. Monk, Martin III. Ogborn, Jon
    370'.7'8   LB1028

    ISBN 0-7099-0698-6

Printed by Antony Rowe Ltd, Chippenham, Wiltshire

CONTENTS

PREFACE

This is not a book in praise of qualitative data, nor is it a critique of the mistakenly or prematurely quantified. It is instead a practical handbook about one method of dealing with and analysing qualitative information in day to day research. It attempts to fill a part of that gap left because, despite many forceful arguments for a more serious approach to the qualitative, there exists less by way of technique when it comes to the actual process of analysis.

The book sets out a notation and a cluster of analytical concepts, and presents substantial examples of them in use in a variety of kinds of research. It offers practical advice to those who want to use the method, and exercises on which to practice technique and deepen understanding. It discusses the main problematic issues the method throws up, in a setting in which it is seen in relation to its relatives in other fields.

There has for too long been too strong an opposition between the qualitative and the quantitative. The task now is not to reinforce one position against the other, but to begin to try to bridge the gulf between them. Happily, much recent work in exploratory quantitative data analysis has a growing sensitivity to the meaning and even the sheer quirkiness of real data. Our own work, starting at the qualitative end of the spectrum, is concerned with one means of confronting the fact that any adequate account of such data must inevitably be in terms of complex and inter-related perceptions, not with a view to quantifying them (though we do not reject that), but with a view to sharpening and clarifying them.

The idea for a book about the analysis of qualitative data took shape in our minds over a number of years. Our first use of the method described in the book was a case of necessity mothering invention, under the urgent pressures of a particular piece of research, but, as others began to try using the method they forced us to become aware of a host of confusions and difficulties. It seemed that the method had some general potential, however, and we began to look for ways of teaching it and to experiment with various ways of using it. Some general principles emerged, and though the process of thinking through the problems can hardly be said to be finished, we began to feel we had something to say.

Some two years ago we persuaded a number of colleagues, to become involved in writing about their experiences of the method. We are indebted to the contributors to the book for their speedy production of drafts, their willingness to meet us to discuss problems, and their tolerance of our editorial changes. Their examples of the method in use are, we feel sure, the most important single thing the book has to offer to educational and other researchers. The ideas and discussion in the rest of the book draw heavily on all these contributions.

We thank a number of people who have given us opportunities to learn about the method by trying to tell others about it. Goery Delacote provided one of us with a month teaching the ideas in Universite Paris VII, and Judah Schwartz a month for two of us at MIT. The University of Neuchatel readily agreed to bi-national supervision of a PhD project, and Francois Grize cheerfully travelled across Europe for meetings and to install his programme.

We thank Jean Knight and Jean Nuttall who filled word processor discs at remarkable speed, with unfailing good humour.

In conclusion, we must record our debt to linguist friends and colleagues. Robin Fawcett has always held that systemic networks could find applications outside linguistics. Ruquaia Hasan and Jim Martin were both generous with criticism and advice. To Michael Halliday we owe most of the fundamental ideas in the book, though he is not to be held responsible for the uses we have made of them.

Joan Bliss   Chelsea College
Martin Monk   Centre for Science and Mathematics Education
Jon Ogborn

PART ONE

FUNDAMENTAL IDEAS

Chapter 1

ABOUT THE BOOK

1.1 ORIGINS

Several years ago, two of us (Joan Bliss and Jon Ogborn) faced with a considerable quantity of qualitative data, set about - with a boldness that in retrospect seems next to foolhardy - adapting a notation used by a group of linguists with whom we were in contact, to the formation of a scheme of descriptive categories for handling that data.   That work (Bliss and Ogborn 1977) some of which is outlined in Chapter 3, led to a number of uses of the notation by colleagues and students (Monk 1977, Mujib 1980, Monk 1981, Grize 1981, Dumas-Carre and Delacote 1981), and so to a gradually growing body of experience.
     It then seemed to a number of those who had used the method, and to others who were interested in it, that it would be useful to collect together some representative samples of uses of the analysis, and to formulate the lessons so far learned, in a practical handbook. This book is the result.

1.2   WHAT IS SYSTEMIC NETWORK ANALYSIS?

Perhaps the main claim made by those whose data is essentially qualitative is that only such data respects the complexity, subtlety and detail of   human transactions.   Without wishing to polarise positions as between kinds of data, it seems to us unarguable that an analysis of qualitative data which does not capture such complexity, subtlety and detail loses much of what the data offers.   However, to state such an ambition is far from being able to fulfill it.   Two strategies are common: one to report results in terms of a relatively simple category scheme, and the other to put before the reader by extensive though necessarily selective quotation the data itself, hoping thus that its essential flavour comes through.
     The kind of analysis suggested here falls between the two.   It works with defined categories, but it attempts to elaborate those categories to the point where enough of the individual essence of data is preserved and represented.   This idea is developed in Section 2.2 of Chapter 2.   The strategy for elaborating categories is to use a

notation - derived from systemic linguistics - which sets out category names in a way that shows their interdependencies. The notation is simple enough, but flexible. It generates network-like structures in which descriptive categories appear linked in a structure which shows, amongst other things, which categories belong within others, which are independent, and which are conditional on the choice of others. One need only leaf through the pages to see a considerable number of examples of such networks.

The method does not provide ready-made schemes of analysis. As a brief inspection of the examples in Chapter 3 will show, each use of the method is individual, producing a network which serves the purposes of that research and does not necessarily have any wider application. It is, however, of course always possible that ideas for an analysis of one problem will prove useful for another.

1.3   STRUCTURE OF THE BOOK

The book falls into four Parts. The first introduces terminology and notation; the second gives nine examples of the use of the method in research; the third provides materials for learning to use the method; and finally the fourth raises and discusses issues and problems associated with it.

The first, introductory Part, consists of the present chapter and Chapter 2. Chapter 2 describes the ideas and notation relatively compactly, and is intended as much for later reference as for an initial exposition.

The examples in Part Two, consisting of Chapter 3, range widely in nature, both in subject matter and in the kind of use they have made of the analysis. The examples will probably communicate better than any more abstract account the possibilities offered by the method, its problems, and its present standing. In it the various contributors indicate their own views of the value and of the difficulties of the method.

Part Three offers material we have found to be useful to those starting to use the method. The chapter of practical advice mentions common difficulties and sources of confusion, and suggests ways we have found to be helpful for developing and improving an analysis. Chapter 5 contains a set of practical exercises which are intended to bring out the most important features of the notation and to provoke reflection on various conceptual difficulties with it. The 'answers' to the exercises consist, not so much of correct solutions, as of a discussion of thoughts each exercise may have brought out.

The final Part, Chapters 6 to 8, discusses the general issues which using the method has exposed. Chapter 6 concerns a variety of difficulties we have found in practice, and ideas about applying the method to various kinds of data. Chapter 7 sketches the relationship of the method to other forms of representation, and Chapter 8 confronts issues of underlying philosophy and of criteria of acceptability.

1.3.1 Using the Book

Whilst it will be difficult to follow the examples without some grasp of the notation and ideas as presented in Chapter 2, it may be helpful to consult a selection of the examples after a first reading of the notation, so as to see something of the way the idea works in practice as soon as possible. The examples are varied, and we hope that each reader will find some that attract their interest.

It is our experience that it is only when one comes to write networks, no matter how trivial the subject matter, that one begins fully to come to grips with the ideas. For this reason, the exercises in Chapter 5 have considerable importance, not merely in practising the use of the tools, but in making one aware of the practical and conceptual problems of using the network apparatus. Having practised using the notation and experienced some of its difficulties, it is likely that the examples in Chapter 3 will appear in a fresh light, and so deserve re-reading at that point.

The remaining chapters can be read in any order, depending on the reader's purposes. Those who wish to attempt to construct a network to describe data of their own will have most need of Chapters 4 and 6, the former intended primarily for beginners and the latter attempting to anticipate some of the range of problems new applications may meet. Both offer forms of possible solutions to a variety of kinds of difficulty.

Those whose purpose is to see network analysis in perspective: to consider the general properties of networks and broad criteria for choosing to use them or not, will find relevant material in Chapters 7 and 8. Chapter 7 deals with formal properties of networks, and compares and contrasts networks with related schemes, from this formal point of view. Chapter 8 attempts to answer some fundamental questions: when one should use a network; what theoretical views they imply; from what the description given by a network derives; and when a network can be judged adequate to its purposes.

1.4 TO WHOM IS THE BOOK ADDRESSED?

This book is primarily written as a practical handbook for those involved in or studying educational and related research. Our own experience is in educational research, and for that reason the focus of the examples is in this field, though we have also selected them for variety so that they range beyond the purely educational.

There is, however, no obvious reason why the methods of network analysis should not be applicable in research in subjects other than education, wherever qualitative data is of importance. Indeed, we took the idea from another discipline. Education borrows from the social sciences most of its methodology, since it deals with the same kind of world seen from its own point of view. Possibly then such a borrowed method may be worth being borrowed back by these same disciplines. It is clearly not for us to make any strong claim of this kind, but it is important to point out the possibility.

1.5   STATUS OF THE IDEAS

The process of writing the book and of discussing draft material with contributors and colleagues, has both helped us to clarify our own ideas and made us aware of remaining areas where further thought and experience is needed.   The appreciable number of applications the method had found gave us some confidence in its potential value, so that a collation of experience and an attempt to draw general lessons from it seemed to be the best way to progress.

We do not regard the method as attached to any strong methodological stance, nor is it particularly linked to any one theoretical position.   Its uses have been rather varied, methodologically and theoretically.   We neither regard the method as an attempt to convert 'soft' data into 'hard', nor as an attempt to get those who prefer the quantitative to look more closely at the qualitative.   We do regard it as a potentially useful tool for clarifying, and for coping with complexity in, one's own schemes of analysis of qualitative data.

We think that the scope for future use of the method is considerable where large bodies of data require analysing at any relatively complex level of detail.   Clearly the method will be too blunt-edged where the need is for a sensitive, delicately shaded and qualified account of human relationships.   Equally it will be too cumbersome when the need is for a few clear descriptive categories. It is our belief that there is a sizeable territory between these two poles, once the potential for exploring it in this way is recognized.

We make no apology for the pragmatic tone of much of the book. Whilst acutely aware of the deeply problematic aspects of dealing with qualitative data, faced at the end of the book, we hold that it is better to develop and to learn about a methodology by using it than purely by thinking about the possibility of using it.   We hope that others may be stimulated to continue the process of extending the range of application of networks, and of thinking about what is involved in doing so.

Chapter 2

NETWORK NOTATION, TERMINOLOGY AND CONCEPTS

2.1 INTRODUCTION

The aim of this chapter is to give a reasonably compact account of the essential ideas of the use of networks for analysing qualitative data. The notation is explained, important terms are defined, and the main concepts discussed and illustrated.

The chapter can be used in two ways. First, it can be used as an introduction to the notation and ideas. It does not, however, attempt to set out any really substantial or important applications, in the interests of brevity and clarity, and the reader will need to turn to later chapters for these. Secondly, the chapter can be used for later reference, if the reader needs to clarify the use of a notation or the meaning of a term or concept.

Simple examples are given of each idea. They have a purely illustrative function, and are not presented as serious attempts at any analysis, nor as complete or even adequate as networks.

Section 2.2 begins by relating analysis using networks to the more familiar simple idea of categorising data, showing that networks can be regarded as a natural extension of straightforward categorisation.

Section 2.3 introduces, in a series of short sub-sections, the essential notation and terminology, to the point where the reader should become able to write his or her own simple networks for describing at least model situations or simple imaginary data.

Section 2.4 discusses the concepts underlying the idea of network analysis, in particular the relations between data, a network and ways of encoding data using a network. Near the end, a sub-section presents such analysis as the construction and use of an artificial language for describing data, which links this section to the next, Section 2.5, which gives a brief account of the origins of the idea in a particular branch of linguistics, and contrasts and compares the linguistic use of networks with that proposed here (see also Chapter 7).

The chapter concludes with a summary Table, showing notation, terms and concepts it introduces, with brief informal glosses indicating the nature of the general ideas which lie behind them.

2.2 CATEGORISING

Networks can usefully be regarded as an extension of the familiar business of putting things into categories. To categorise is to attach a label to things; in effect to place them in boxes. A network can be seen as a map of the set of boxes one has chosen to use, which shows how they relate to one another. The set of relationships can be arbitrarily complex.

We want to suggest that appropriate analyses of qualitative data can be thought of as stretching along a continuum, at the extremes of which the network idea is either pointless or irrelevant, but with a broad middle range in which the idea has something to offer.

One extreme is that at which every item of data is best regarded as unique and individual, in need of an account proper only to it itself, in which any description which might apply to other things has to be carefully qualified to tailor it to the particular case. This will often be true when one is working with individual case-studies of people, institutions or events, where nothing less complex or finely nuanced than a carefully and sympathetically written prose account will do. Obvious examples might include the history of a school, the workings of a curriculum development project, or the life-histories of a set of people. At this extreme, one is mainly concerned to avoid any hard-edged set of categories: to set up stereotypes only at once to undermine them.

The opposite extreme is that at which data falls naturally into simple and unproblematic groupings, or when the best strategy is to act as if it does. Thus solutions to problems might be classified as correct, incorrect, or incomplete; students as belonging to different years of study; school subjects as falling into groups such as science or humanities; people as categorised into social classes by the Registrar General's classification. But even to mention examples raises immediate doubts, few if any being as simple as they are being made to be. The simplicity of such sets of boxes or labels owes more to research strategy than to clear divisions in reality.

When one is concerned with rather more fidelity, category schemes soon become more complex, and it is as the desirable level of complexity rises that networks begin to find their use. Figure 2.1 shows schematically two kinds of added complexity, with their translations into network notation. Thus Figure 2.1(b) suggests how a simple scheme of exclusive categories all at one level as shown in Figure 2.1(a) might be elaborated so that each category contains sub-categories, perhaps varying in number and depth. The natural representation is of a set of nested boxes. Figure 2.1(c) shows a different kind of elaboration, which can arise when it becomes necessary to describe the same data from more than one point of view, so that each item of data is simultaneously classified with respect to different aspects. Clearly the two kinds of elaboration can be, and often are, combined.

Figure 2.1 is purely schematic: the letters A, B, C etc. stand for meaningful category names in some particular analysis: see later examples in Section 2.3.

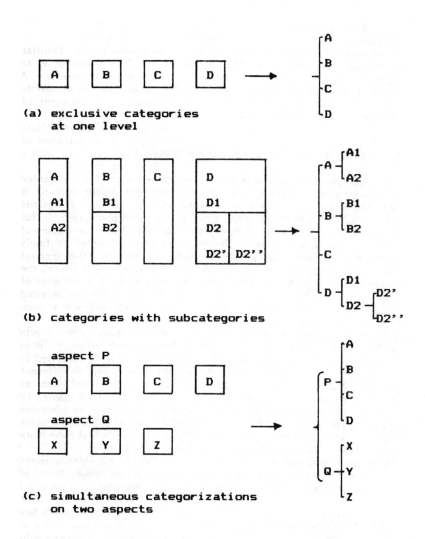

(a) exclusive categories
    at one level

(b) categories with subcategories

(c) simultaneous categorizations
    on two aspects

Figure 2.1   Category schemes and related networks.

9

What we are saying is very simple. To categorise is to draw distinctions and to name them, recognising that distinctions may need to be drawn along several independent dimensions, and that any distinction may need to be further divided into subsidiary divisions. Networks offer a uniform notation to express such schemes at any required level of complexity, and a terminology intended to clarify and assist communication of the issues involved. At this level all they do is formalise the obvious.

2.3 NETWORK NOTATION AND TERMINOLOGY

The purely notational aspects of writing networks are both simple and straightforward. Networks as used here are constructed using just a few elementary notations; two indicating kinds of choice or selection, one indicating constraints or conditions on choices, and one indicating the possibility of repeated choice.

In the sections which follow, each will be introduced with examples, together with the terminology we have found useful for describing the structure, content and rationale of networks. The examples used here for illustration are deliberately obvious, even banal, so as to focus attention as far as possible on the mechanics of the network notation and away from what it is being used to do. In Chapter 3, by contrast, the notation and terminology is taken for granted, and attention is directed to the actual use of networks for a variety of different problems. Some readers may find it useful to look at a few of the examples in Chapter 3 at an early stage, using the present chapter purely for reference for the meanings of technical terms. Some may find it helpful while reading this chapter to turn also to the exercises in Chapter 5, to test their understanding.

The introduction here has to work at three levels. At the lowest level there is simply the notation we have chosen to use. At the next level is a set of defined technical terms, needed in order to give a clear and consistent account of what a network is doing. Above both is the level of simple general ideas about classifying and encoding data which gives the network system its rationale, and which the system is intended to clarify, develop or sharpen.

2.3.1 Terms, Systems, Bar

Any category scheme needs names for categories. We shall usually use English words, for their mnemonic or suggestive value, though sometimes contracted words or arbitrary symbols will be more convenient. All such category names we shall call **terms**. They are the words which appear in the networks, at all levels. A network links terms so as to specify the possible choices amongst them.

Given any category, it is usually not too difficult to think of plausible subdivisions. Thus we can divide schools into, say, state and private, into primary and secondary, or into single-sex and co-educational. Figure 2.2 illustrates these subcategorisations, and

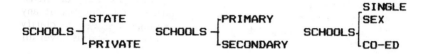

Figure 2.2   Three different systems describing
             schools.

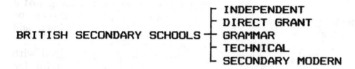

Figure 2.3   A system with five terms.

shows the BAR notation, consisting of a vertical line with the main category to the left and the subcategories to the right, which is used to indicate such cases.

Notice that each pair of choices has a certain coherence, being a distinction along some meaningful dimension, whether of status, age-range or entry characteristics.   Both terms in any pair each get some of their meaning by the contrast they make with the other.   We shall call any such coherent set of terms a **system**, when the sub-categories it presents are mutually exclusive and at least help to define one another by the contrasts they mutually offer.

The number of subcategories to the right of a bar is not restricted to two.   The number used depends entirely on the nature of the material being analysed, and on the analyst's knowledge, theories or feelings about what would most make sense.   Thus for some purposes, the simple dichotomy of state versus private schools in Figure 2.2 might be elaborated into the larger set, running from independent to secondary modern shown in Figure 2.3.

At the simple general level, the notation expresses the idea of a single large category divided along some important dimension into smaller, mutually exclusive categories.   The terms in such a finite system are mnemonic names for categories, which - though having external criteria -   also define each other by exclusion: for the purposes of the analysis a grammar school is that which is not any of the other kinds.   The bar is the simple notation for any such set of exclusive choices.

The following sections show how this idea, whilst perfectly obvious, is when combined with others not quite as trivial as it looks.

2.3.2 Delicacy, Terminals

Subcategories can clearly have their own sub-subcategories: correspondingly terms on a bar can lead to further systems, so generating a tree as illustrated in Figure 2.4, which attempts a rough and ready map of a typical British secondary school curriculum.

As one passes down any branch of the tree, the distinctions become finer and finer. We shall call this an increase in **delicacy**, so that down any branch there are successive levels of delicacy. Equally, moving back up the tree one moves to less and less delicate distinctions.

Thus in Figure 2.4, the curriculum is divided into five least delicate categories. One of them, HUMANITIES, is then distinguished at the next level of delicacy into LANGUAGES and SOCIETY, the former being yet more delicately distinguished into LIVING languages and CLASSICAL languages, and finally LIVING languages divided into MOTHER TONGUE and OTHER living languages.

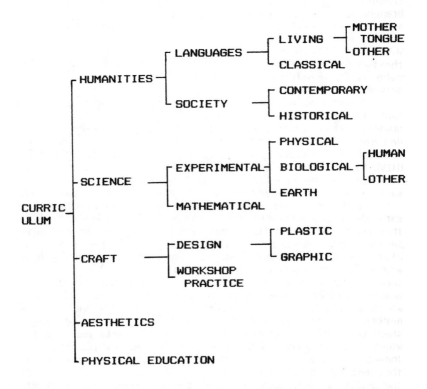

FIGURE 2.4 A network showing increasing delicacy.

There are terms, beyond which no further distinctions are made. This most delicate set of terms we shall call **terminals.** Notice that terminals appear at different levels of delicacy in different branches of the tree: AESTHETICS has no further development beyond the least delicate level; the EXPERIMENTAL science branch is developed to two further levels while MATHEMATICAL science terminates at that level.

Notice that terminals, and all terms more delicate than the least inherit properties back up branches of the tree. HUMAN means human biology; BIOLOGICAL is EXPERIMENTAL, and like PHYSICAL and EARTH is a science, at any rate as these matters are represented in Figure 2.4. So too is GRAPHIC art shown as belonging to DESIGN and through that to CRAFT.

We have defined level of delicacy only with respect to individual branches of a tree. It follows that in any one branch, it is at least good practice, and should perhaps be regarded as an obligation, that terms in a system at any particular level should have roughly the same coarseness or fineness of distinction. Thus for example, in the SCIENCE branch, we would like the triplet PHYSICAL science, BIOLOGICAL science, and EARTH science to represent distinctions at a roughly similar level, with the distinction between EXPERIMENTAL and MATHEMATICAL science operating at a less delicate level, but with the two being again comparable. To suggest this is at once to make clear that delicacy is relative to the intention of the network.

There may, or there may not, be an implication in a tree such as Figure 2.4 that terms at the same levels in different branches (and so in Figure 2.4 vertically aligned) are equally delicate. One might, for example, consider that the distinctions between LANGUAGES and SOCIETY within HUMANITIES, and between EXPERIMENTAL and MATHEMATICAL SCIENCE, are similar in delicacy. It is less clear that such a position could be maintained at all levels.

As soon as one inspects a network such as this with any care, objections and difficulties appear. An obvious case is the position of the MOTHER TONGUE, English, which appears as a terminal, most delicate term, but could well be regarded as one of the main, and so least delicate divisions of the curriculum, and indeed has a relation, not shown by the network, to the gross term AESTHETICS. It is not our present purpose to argue such points, nor does the network present a view of the curriculum to which we are committed. What we intend is to show that a network, through the choice of levels of delicacy (and as we shall see later through other choices) does present such a view, which by being presented becomes open to argument and criticism. Indeed, it cannot be too strongly stressed, even at this stage, that nothing in the notation or terminology of networks, tells the analyst what to do with them: what terms to choose, where in delicacy to stop, and so on. These are matters of decision and judgment. The network just displays the consequences.

2.3.3 Co-selection, Bra

The three different systems shown in Figure 2.2 could all apply simultaneously to a school. That is, it could be at once STATE or PRIVATE, PRIMARY or SECONDARY, and SINGLE-SEX or CO-EDUCATIONAL. Figure 2.5 shows a notation which expresses this possibility.

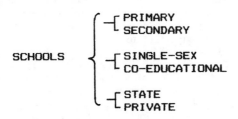

Figure 2.5   Illustration of bracket

The bracket, abbreviated to BRA, in the figure indicates that selections must be made in all the systems which follow the bracket. Where the BAR indicates mutually exclusive categories, the BRA indicates necessary co-selection. On reaching a BRA at any level in a network, one pursues all the systems which develop from it, making category selections as indicated by their structure in each system.

The general idea notated by a BRA and expressed in the term co-selection is simply that situations to be described will often have a number of distinct and independent aspects all needing to be represented.

The network of Figure 2.5 says that a school can be given any one of the following eight compound descriptions:

primary co-educational state school
primary co-educational private school
primary single-sex state school
primary single-sex private school
secondary co-educational state school
secondary co-educational private school
secondary single-sex state school
secondary single-sex private school

Figure 2.6(a) shows a second example of co-selection, this time to do with different kinds of sums in arithmetic.

The network is again straightforward. Sums can involve adding, subtracting, multiplying or dividing, any of which can be done on integers or on real numbers. Note the possibility of describing ADDITIVE sums on (say) INTEGERS, thus embracing both addition and subtraction. One need not attend only to terminal features in forming descriptions.

We remark again that a network cannot avoid presenting a view of the material it describes. Subtraction and division could have, for example, been presented as inverse operations, as in Figure 2.6(b). To represent multiplication and division being carried out additively using logarithms would require a more radical reformulation. Other operands, such as fractions, rational or irrational, could be included.

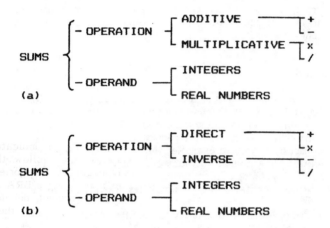

Figure 2.6 (a) Co-selections describing sums
(b) Alternative to (a)

OPERATION	DIRECT		INVERSE	
OPERAND	+	x	−	/
INTEGERS				
REAL NUMBERS				

Figure 2.7 Contingency table for network in Figure 2.6(b)

Terms or systems following a bracket are analogous to the different dimensions of a contingency table. Thus Figure 2.7 shows the table corresponding to the network of Figure 2.6(b). Similarly, the description of schools in the network of Figure 2.5 yields a 2x2x2 table, with eight cells each corresponding to one of the previously listed school descriptions.

It follows that a network using brackets can often be a compact way of representing the structure of data one has collected, or intends to collect, particularly when a considerable number of dimensions is involved.

Further, the computer program BARBARA (see Appendix A) will accept a network as specifying a contingency table, and will report as requested counts of cases specified by given collections of terms, corresponding to counts in various cells, collapsed across certain variables if required. See also Appendix B on the analysis of contingency tables.

2.3.4 Recursion

So far it has been implied that a categorical description is formed by passing once and once only through a network. There are cases where it is more economical to allow repeated selections in part, or even all, of a network. This we call **recursion**.

Suppose, by way of an example, that we want to represent levels of qualification in a number of subjects, such as O-level in English, A-level in History, and a first degree in Geography. Figure 2.8 shows the recursion notation which simplifies drawing networks in such cases.

The circular arrow at the entry to the BRA indicates that one may pass through the bracket as many times as are necessary, each time making one of the possible sets of selections. This generates a string of categories, so that one person may be described as having pre-O-level in English and O-level in Mathematics, while another may have A-level in English and A-level in History.

Recursion may be regarded as a shorthand for a more elaborate notation, in which a BRA contains a choice of whether to stop or recur, as shown in Figure 2.9.

It is often not necessary to use recursion, and doing so may, while making the network more compact and elegant, hide something one would prefer to be more visible. Figures 2.10(a) and (b) compare two networks describing modes of transport. In (a) recursion is used to allow for vehicles, such as hovercraft, which are not restricted to just one of the media land, sea or air. In (b) the various combinations are spelt out, which both makes them explicit, and suggests deleting combinations that are implausible (such perhaps as the universal land/sea/air vehicle). In the previous example, one might want to do the same if combinations such as O-level Philosophy are known to be impossible.

Recursion can be used, as in the two examples given here, with both BRA and BAR.

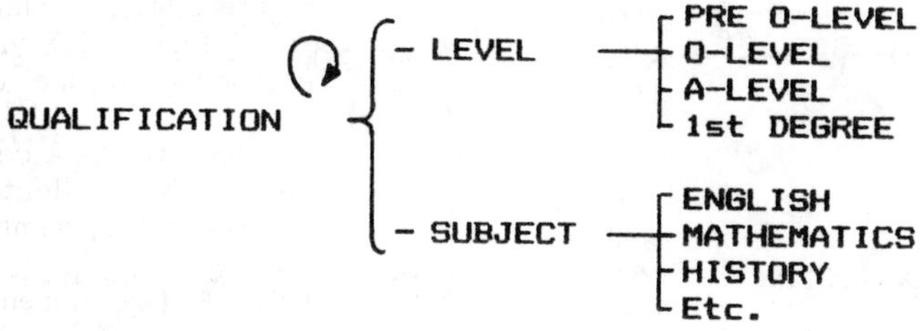

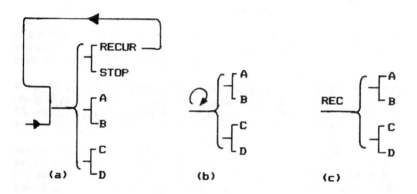

Figure 2.8 Levels of qualification,
using a recursive bracket.

Figure 2.9 Recursion (a) with STOP or RECUR
(b),(c) simplified notations.

Recursion with a BAR is easy to confuse with the use of a simple BRA. Thus the network of Figure 2.10(c) seems to do much the same job as the recursive part of Figure 2.10(a). The difference is that it insists on, for example representing LAND as LAND NOT-SEA NOT-AIR and it allows NOT-LAND NOT-SEA NOT-AIR which may or may not make sense (a space craft?).

Recursion expresses the idea that ordinarily exclusive categories may sometimes apply in combination; co-selection that there are several aspects of a thing which all need to be described. A linguistic example of recursion appears in Section 2.5.

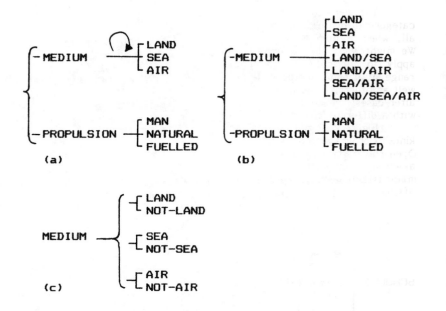

Figure 2.10 Transportation (a) using recursion (b) avoiding recursion (c) using a BRA in place of the recursion in (a).

2.3.5 Restrictive Entry Conditions

The bracket notation 'says' that all choices in the systems which follow it can co-occur. Actual data, or situations to be described, are not always so simple, or so tolerant of some allowed combinations. Thus it may have occurred to the reader that in the network of Figure 2.5, there is a difficulty with the description of private primary schools, in that the private sector, while it has primary schools of the age range 5-11 as does the state sector, has also the system of preparatory schools. The category 'preparatory school' simply does not arise in the state sector, so the network of Figure 2.5 cannot be amended just by adding PREP to the system containing PRIMARY and SECONDARY.

Figure 2.11 illustrates the use of restrictive entry conditions, here to allow PREP schools only in the PRIVATE sector. The notation is a reversed bracket, which it is convenient to abbreviate to CON (for 'conditions'). The systems which follow such an entry condition bracket are entered only when all the terms which lead into the reversed bracket have previously been selected. If all have been selected, then the systems that follow must be entered.

The general idea expressed by CON is that some kinds of categorical distinctions only arise, indeed may only have sense at all, when a number of rather different conditions are satisfied. We might want, for example, very different kinds of distinctions to apply to curricula in different kinds of school, especially if the range of schools included is (say) special or progressive schools as well as others. So entry conditions are needed when circumstances alter cases; when the network for one kind of thing has to develop with a different structure from that for another.

Figure 2.12 gives a small example, showing some of the special kinds of programme on various television channels. Only BBC2 shows Open University programmes; only BBC2 has news with subtitles as well as without; only BBC1 educational programmes include programmes in minority languages, and programmes for the hobbyist. With the advent of Channel Four it is already out of date.

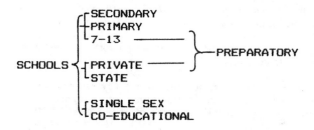

Figure 2.11   Amended Figure 2.5, illustrating use of
restrictive entry conditions.

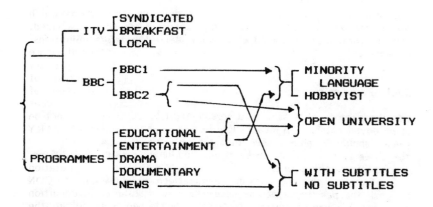

Figure 2.12   Network for TV programmes, illustrating
use of several entry conditions.

CON can have any number of inputs, not merely two. The normal structure of a network looks after the case of one necessary condition: note in Figure 2.12 how the distinction SYNDICATED or LOCAL arises only for ITV, without need for further notation.

2.3.6 Summary of Notation and Terminology

In Sections 2.3.1 to 2.3.5 we have introduced:

terms as names of categories, organised in **systems** each offering an exclusive choice, indicated by the BAR notation.

successive systems, of increasing **delicacy** or fineness of distinction, as far as the **terminals.**

simultaneous description of independent aspects, using **co-selection** from several systems, notated with the bracket or BRA, and the analogy of this with contingency tables.

recursion, used when all or part of a network needs to be applied more than once.

compound **entry conditions,** notated with a reverse bracket or CON, needed when different combinations of categories lead to different kinds of further systems of categories.

Table 2.1 at the end of the chapter summarises the terms, notation, and also the network concepts to be discussed in Section 2.4.

2.4 NETWORK CONCEPTS

One general network concept, that of delicacy, has already been introduced (2.3.2). The sections which follow introduce some further concepts, which prove useful in thinking about the nature and uses of networks.

2.4.1 Paradigms

For the purpose of a survey, a person might be described as a white, unemployed youth. Another might be a white, employed adult. The reader should be able to see that the network in Figure 2.13 allows the three pairs of terms to be freely combined, giving eight possible descriptive combinations.

We shall call the allowed combinations of terms for any given network the **paradigms** of the network. In Figure 2.13 one of the eight possible paradigmatic selections of terms has been indicated by highlighting three of the terms. The use of the term paradigm in this context derives from linguistics (see 2.5). We propose to retain it, in its sense of 'pattern' or 'possible choice amongst alternatives', despite the potential confusion with its recently current use (and sometimes abuse) in the post-Kuhnian discussion of alternative research programmes. Our use of the term is essentially neutral, and carries no overtones concerning any analysis of research methodology.

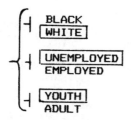

Figure 2.13   A network with one paradigm selected

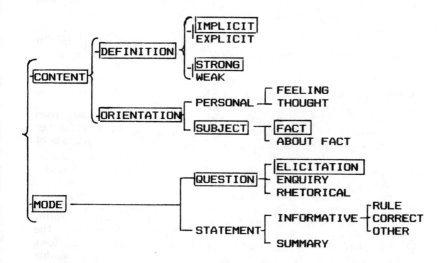

Figure 2.14   Network describing teachers utterances.

21

Consider next a more complicated example. Figure 2.14 proposes a network intended to describe teachers' classroom utterances. Each utterance is described as having a certain CONTENT and MODE. The CONTENT is described as having more or less explicitness and strength of definition, and also PERSONAL or SUBJECT ORIENTATION. The MODEs are distinguished into QUESTION or STATEMENT, these being differentiated more delicately as shown.

This network presents no fewer than 112 paradigms (2 x 2 definitions x 4 orientations x 7 modes). Just one, in which the teacher is described as eliciting a fact in a strongly defined but implicit way, has been picked out as previously. It becomes clear from the figure that a paradigm can be thought of as the trace of a path through the network (and could equally well be represented by highlighting the lines connecting the selected terms).

An immediate test of any network is whether each and every paradigm makes good sense, in terms of the intentions of the analysis. Is the possibility, allowed by this network, of a rhetorical question about a personal feeling, strongly and explicitly defined, a sensible combination? Perhaps, 'Are you feeling especially tired today?', asked in an ironic tone of a child who often does little work, might serve as an instance. What about summary statements of personal feelings, however defined? This category seems to be present mainly to deal with the giving of factual information, though, 'I know we all hate this but it's got to be done' might be defended as an instance.

The point here is not to criticise this particular network, but to bring out that any network needs to be adjusted until all its paradigms can be defended as making sense. They constitute the finite set of allowed descriptions, and no possible description should be nonsense.

The general idea behind the technical notion of a paradigm is simply that any description of something is what it is, against the background of what it might have been. To call a book difficult or a play very long implies that the book could have been easier and the play shorter. In ordinary discourse, the background of alternatives may be large and diffuse. In the analysis of data using networks, it is finite and well-defined, though not necessarily small or unsubtle. It is part of the point of using networks that a reasonably compact network, say twice as large as Figure 2.14, can express a rather large number of finely differentiated descriptions. Further, these descriptions are not simply listed, but are co-ordinated so as to show where and how they have something in common with others.

Given any set of data, say people's accounts of their work, one usually feels that it has some overall coherence or pattern, with individual accounts being variations, large or small, on a number of themes. The idea of a network is to capture this overall structure, with its paradigms corresponding to individual items within that structure.

2.4.2 Code, Realisation

One will often want to write some coded version of the description of each item of data. For computer coding, for example, it has been common to enter strings of digits, such as 1=male 2=female; 1=married 2=unmarried; etc.

There are several ways of encoding the paradigms taken from a network, which assign descriptions to data. Perhaps the worst way one could imagine would be to list all the paradigms and give each a number, using the number as the code. That would be economical, but not at all expressive.

Another way would be simply to copy all the terms selected in the paradigm, usually with parentheses to indicate the relations between them. Thus the paradigm selected in Figure 2.14 might be encoded as:

```
(CONTENT (DEFINITION (IMPLICIT STRONG)
          ORIENTATION (SUBJECT (FACT)))
  MODE (QUESTION (ELICITATION)))
```

This we shall call **extended code.** It will often be convenient to abbreviate some or all terms. If the words chosen for terms make the code read somewhat like a meaningful sentence in a kind of telegraphic English, so much the better.

However, some words in an extended code are redundant. In the above example, CONTENT, MODE, DEFINITION and ORIENTATION will appear always, and so can be understood. Further, any ELICITATION must, because it belongs to a system coming after the term QUESTION, be preceded by QUESTION in the code, so such cases can also be left to be understood. It follows that anyone who knows the network can recover the complete description if just given the terminal items. For the example above we get just:

IMPLICIT STRONG FACT ELICITATION

This we shall call **brief code.** As described in Appendix A, the computer programme BARBARA will accept both kinds of code, but because it also stores the network, it can trace all the implications of the brief form.

Of course any rules, whatever they are, which produce a unique code for each paradigm will serve to code data. A network might represent positive and negative feelings of various kinds, and the rule might be to insert 'NOT' in the code in just the negative case, giving, say HAPPY, NOT HAPPY, INTERESTED, NOT INTERESTED, etc. If the network drew a distinction between fairly certain and rather dubious cases one might insert a query '?' in the code for the latter. One might even use rules about word order to encode a difference, as in WORK IS USEFUL versus IS WORK USEFUL.

We shall call the set of rules, whatever they may be, that turn paradigms into codes, the code **realisation rules.** For extended code, the realisation rule is essentially 'copy all terms in the paradigm'. For brief code, the rule is simply 'copy the terminals'.

We emphasise the concept of code realisation rule because, when codes are expressed by copying terminals, it is easy to confuse the code with the paradigm. The code is any convenient way of writing down the paradigm structure. The paradigm itself is the more abstract notion of some pattern selected from other possible other patterns. Their relation is not unlike that between 'what I'm thinking' and 'what I say'.

2.4.3   Instantiation, Representation

Data is one thing, and descriptions of it, however complex or subtle, are another. The description can not, and should not try to, capture everything. Furthermore, the description has some ulterior motive which the data does not share: in a word, an analysis is a limited view chosen for a purpose.

The paradigms of a network, then, represent that set of discriminations which suits the analyst, and which he or she thinks suits the job in hand. Nevertheless, data is rarely so kind as to reflect exactly what one would like to see there so one has an inevitable problem of deciding about the goodness of match of description to data.

We have already pointed out (2.4.1) the need to test all the paradigms of a network to check that each could in principle correspond to some item of data. That is, one needs to check for possible **instances** of each. An instance of a paradigm is a possible item of data that fits the description assigned by the paradigm. It is all too easy to generate paradigms which could not possibly have instances - social interactions between one person, for example.

Equally, there will normally be items of data which one does not want to ignore, which are given bad, incomplete or non-existent descriptions by a given network. That is, they are not **represented** adequately, or at all, by any one of the existing paradigms.

The general idea is simply that to be any good, a descriptive scheme ought to be coherent and sensible, and ought to cover all the important material to be described. Failures of instantiation or representation are two main diagnostic tools in the improvement of networks.

2.4.4   Rank

We use the term **rank**, also borrowed from linguists, to refer to the 'size' of chunks of data which are treated as each getting a coded description via a network. So far we have avoided this question, referring to 'data' as though it was obvious just what needed analysis.

Consider some examples, however. Suppose the data concerns the organisational structure of schools. Will one choose to construct a network to make distinctions, such as 'hierarchical' or 'devolved' which distinguish different kinds of total structure, or will one choose to describe smaller elements of that structure, such as 'faculty' or 'department' or 'service section', together perhaps with their relationships to one another? In the first case, the network categories make distinctions about the whole; in the second such differences would emerge as different patternings in descriptions of the arrangement of the parts. The difference is like that between distinguishing, on the one hand, between television and radio, and on the other, between devices with or without aerials, amplifiers, loudspeakers, and cathode-ray tubes. One describes at the rank of the whole device, the other at the rank of main component.

Another example might be data concerning problem-solving. The networks in Figure 2.15 differ in the size of units they analyse, though not very much in their general approach.

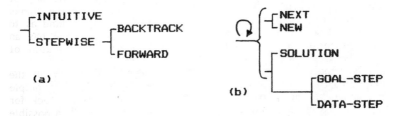

Figure 2.15 Two networks about problem solving, differing with respect to rank.

The first network attempts to describe the solution as a whole; classing it as either arrived at in one 'flash of insight' or step by step, the latter being divided into steps which work backwards from the goal ('backward reasoning') or forwards by inferences from given information. The second attempts to represent the solution process as a string of moves, with two simple links, NEXT for a step following the last and NEW for a fresh start. Codes for each look rather different. The first network has just three paradigms, with extended codes:

INTUITIVE
STEPWISE (BACKTRACK)
STEPWISE (FORWARD)

Each whole solution would get one such description, though nothing prevents it being made more extensive and complex. By contrast, the second network produces a sequence of steps, for example:

```
((NEW DATA-STEP)
 (NEXT GOAL-STEP)
 (NEXT DATA-STEP)
 (NEXT SOLUTION))
```

corresponding to some mixture of the kinds of step defined by network 2.15(a). There might be any number, in any order. The process previously coded as INTUITIVE could now appear as the single step NEW SOLUTION.

The example merely illustrates the general idea that what is to count as an individual item of data is a matter of decision. That decision depends on the kind of pattern or structure one is looking for. A number of contrasting examples can be found in Chapter 3.

2.4.5 Description Language

Any set of categories, however simple, is in some sense a language for describing data. If we divide people into five social classes, we have chosen a 'language' with five 'words' in which descriptive 'sentences' are all just one word long. In such a case, the notion of a description language is little more than a conceit.

The idea is less fanciful if we consider a network, its paradigms, and their coded versions. The network defines well-formed descriptive structures (the paradigms), and we can regard the codes as sentences in a language whose structures of meaning are given by the network. Less abstractly, one writes a network to organise the kinds of thing one wants to say about given data, and uses it to say what needs saying about each item of data.

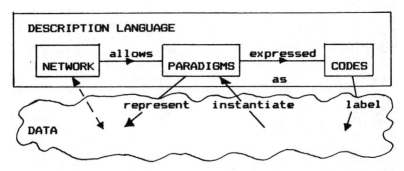

Figure 2.16   A network as an artificial description
              language.

Figure 2.16 pictures the idea. To construct a network and use it to encode data is like constructing an artificial language, which offers meanings and distinctions of the kind one wants, and then using it to give an account of data in those terms. The language is entirely the analyst's own responsibility: it can as easily be unperceptive as perceptive, irrelevant as relevant, over- or under-detailed as well-chosen. All that networks offer is a notation with which to do one's best, which exposes the choices made for further thought.

2.4.6 Flexibility

We have so far, in the interests of clarity, taken a rather rigid - even formalist - approach. We have done our best to define notation, terms and concepts as unambiguously as we can.

This should not be taken as any indication of an insistence on rigidity. Indeed, many of the ideas discussed and defined here have arisen out of thinking about the implications of various ad-hoc strategies we have used or seen being used.

For this reason, we would be the first to encourage people to use the network ideas and notation as flexibly as they wish, if necessary giving things their own interpretation or adding their own notations: To give one or two examples, one might find it useful to develop several different networks for different aspects of data, and leave their connection with one another undecided, or one might have a network which developed not from one starting point but from several.

2.5 ORIGIN OF NETWORKS IN SYSTEMIC LINGUISTICS

The content of this chapter so far has presented what must seem a formidable, perhaps unnecessary amount of terminology and notation. It is not of course, our own invention: it has been largely taken from other sources. The purpose of the present section is to acknowledge and clarify that debt.

2.5.1 Systemic Linguistics

Our main source has been that school of linguistics known as systemic linguistics (see References). Deriving in general from one of the founding fathers of modern linguistics, de Saussure, specifically from the British linguist Firth, and influenced by the anthropologist Malinowski, is the idea that meaning in language has essentially to do with choice in context. That is, a word or phrase does not 'contain' its meaning as a bucket contains water, but has the meaning it does by being the choice, in a given context, that it is and by so excluding the choices that it might have been. Less abstractly, in the context of starting a letter, "Dear Mary" is a choice of friendly informality, being that by at the same time not being either "Dear Mrs Black" or

"Darling Mary".

The systemic linguists, primarily Halliday, elaborated this simple idea from which clearly derives the concept, due to them, of a system. One extension takes account of the obvious fact that in language we often mean more than one thing at once - there is not one expression for each meaning. A clear case is that of gender and number in French: 'grand', 'grande', 'grands', 'grandes'. Each is a choice along two dimensions at once - hence the idea of co-selection and the bracket notation.

In fact, the systemic linguists largely concern themselves, not with grammatical minutae, but with wider and deeper problems of meaning, such as the way a child acquires the adult meaning system, with meaning changes in sub-culture languages, or with the way phrases cohere into extended meaningful texts or utterances. For this reason, their linguistic ideas already looked quite close to what one might need in order to handle data such as an interview transcript.

We have borrowed from them the bar, bracket and entry condition bracket notations and the terms term, system, delicacy, recursion, paradigm, realisation, and rank. There are, however, some radical differences which arise from our very different purposes. In particular, an analysis of qualitative data, in the sense we propose, is not in any sense a linguistic analysis. If it were, it would be better to turn directly to linguistics for help. For the same reason, the utility of the borrowed notation and terminology does not depend on the rightness or wrongness of the linguistic theory from which it came (see also Chapter 7).

The essential difference in approach is that the linguist is interested in what instances of language in use reveal about the structure of the language itself, be it English, French or Chinese, while the educational researcher is interested in what data, which may just happen to be spoken or written, can reveal or suggest about questions of a different kind, such as what people believe or how they learned something.

Thus a systemic linguist's network will attempt to account for language structures. For example (see Kress 1976) Halliday has proposed that the pattern of tense in English is not simply present, past and future with a few compounds, but is essentially recursive. The idea is that tenses are formed by recursive selection from the choices about-past, about-present, about-future. Examples include:

about past: e.g. took/did take
about past about future: e.g. was going to take
about past about future about present:
    e.g. was going to be taking

reaching complexities like 'will have been going to have been taking' (about future about past about future about past about present) as in "You will have been going to have been starting every day this week soon", said ironically to a reluctant author who keeps intending to begin.

By contrast, the analyst of qualitative data is not using, but is instead manufacturing a language for his or her own purposes. A network can offer a tool kit, but not the content or design. All the tool kit essentially imports from linguistics is the idea that meanings are given by contrasts in given contexts, and that complex meanings can be built out of parallel contrasts with respect to different aspects. The rest is pure invention to suit the data one confronts.

GENERAL IDEA	TECHNICAL TERM	NOTATION
Category name; thing picked out	term	e.g. BOY
Finest category or distinction made	terminal	e.g. TINY
Choice; difference in context of alternatives	system	BAR ⊣[
Parallel aspects; simultaneous choices	co-selection	BRA {
Circumstances alter cases; restriction; constraints	entry condition	CON }
Repeated possibilities	recursion	REC ↻
Greater fineness of distinction	delicacy	tree structures
One from many possible patterns	paradigm	path in a network
Saying what is in an item of data	code	FRIEND(CLOSE)
Handy expression for a category	realisation rule	e.g. copy terminals
Example in data of a category	instantiation	
How categories deal with data	representation	
Size, scale, unit of things described	rank	
Finding a reasonable way to talk about data	description language	

Table 2.1   Summary of Ideas, Terms and Notation

PART TWO

NETWORKS IN USE

Chapter 3

EXAMPLES OF THE USE OF NETWORKS

We feel sure that the best way to appreciate the potential uses of the network method is through examples of its use. Thus this chapter, representing a substantial part of the book, offers nine cases of its application to a variety of kinds of research problem. All but one have been written by the researchers involved.

The examples, grouped together for further discussion, are:

3.1 Joan Bliss
Students' reactions to learning.
3.2 Janet Holland
Childrens' classifications:
using a network developed by another.
3.3 Tony Orgee
Perceptions of pupil performance.

3.4 Nancy Johnson
Using networks to represent Karen's knowledge of maths.
3.5 Martin Monk
A network description of comments on peers.

3.6 Paul Black, Harry Elliott
Problem solving by chemistry students.
3.7 D. Michael Watts
Using networks to represent pupils' meanings
for the concepts of force and energy.
3.8 Jon Ogborn
Use of a network for item banking.

3.9 Martin Monk, Jon Ogborn
Language development and the language of control.

The first group (3.1 to 3.3) are of broad educational interest. Joan Bliss reports on what was in fact our first substantial use of networks, on a type of problem many will share, namely data consisting of descriptions by people of events and of their feelings about them. Such 'story data' is both valuable and intractable. Janet Holland describes work done in the Sociological Research Unit of the University of London Institute of Education, in which the use of networks was taken for granted as a means of handling coding frames. Tony Orgee gives an account of a typical kind of use of qualitative data, namely to inform and deepen an understanding of quantitative data, here results of surveys by the Assessment of Performance Unit.

The second group (3.4, 3.5) form a contrasting pair. Nancy Johnson's use of networks was concerned with the problem of the accurate description of the knowledge of just one child. Her network offers a picture of one individual. Martin Monk, on the other hand, shows how he used a network to deal with a large bulk of simple qualitative data; pupils' comments on their classmates. His is an example where the network analysis can lead to a later stage of statistical analysis of category frequencies.

The third group (3.6 to 3.8) all concern problems in research in science education. Paul Black and Harry Elliott discuss two kinds of use of networks in one piece of work: to map the scientific concepts and relations used in solving a problem, and to follow in some detail the processes of problem solving. Michael Watts, like Nancy Johnson (3.4), is concerned with describing the knowledge of individuals, but also with the problems of generalising beyond individuals to describe typical clusterings of ideas often held by pupils about force and energy. Jon Ogborn's example starts with the advantage of a well-structured body of scientific knowledge taken as given, and describes how a network can be used to generate descriptions of the knowledge content of test questions.

In the final example (3.9) we describe at secondhand two further uses of networks. One is a study by Michael Halliday of the early language development of a child, with successive networks representing a changing grammar. The other is a sociolinguistic study by Geoffrey Turner of language used to control behaviour. Their presence in the book helps to acknowledge our debt to systemic linguistics.

Neither we nor the authors of the various examples would regard all of them as having equal standing. Some are more tentative and exploratory than others, their interest for the book being precisely that in this way some of the difficulties of using networks can be exposed for consideration. We have tried to collect examples of as wide a variety as possible, from amongst those known to us, so as both to bring out the very different ways in which networks can be used, and to illustrate the range of advantages they present and the difficulties they give rise to, in a variety of contexts.

3.1 STUDENTS' REACTIONS TO LEARNING

by Joan Bliss

3.1.1 Introduction

We first made use of networks as an answer to the problem of analysing some 300 rambling stories, which came from asking students to tell us about times when learning at university felt particularly good or particularly bad. With a well worked out interview, and a little encouragement from the interviewer, we found that students were willing to talk freely about such experiences: as a result transcripts of a story were often several pages long.

How then were we to manage the sheer bulk of the data? Over and above the quantity of material we were also struck by the fact that no two stories were alike; that each had its own highly individualistic quality. Our first approach was necessarily very simple. We classified the different types of situations about which students talked, such as lectures, laboratories, working on their own, and tutorials, and we looked at bad and good stories in these groups. This simple classification, although a useful first shot, missed a great deal of the detail concerning why students experienced good or bad feelings about learning.

To go further, we attempted a more detailed classification of the feelings described by students. In doing so we became more aware of the great diversity of these feelings and also of the very wide range of reasons given for them. No simple classifications seemed to capture the complex picture being painted by students. It was at this point that we turned to constructing networks, hoping that they would permit us to organise a large set of descriptive categories into a structured system.

To think about constructing networks we had somehow to organise the huge amount of unstructured data in the students' stories. Features that had something in common with each other needed to be grouped together, and we decided that a structured informal summary of the story would enable us to do this. So in each summary we followed the same pattern of answering the following three questions:

What situation does the story concern?
What did the student feel?
Why did the student have those feelings?

The general process of network construction was as follows. The informal summaries provided the material that could be used as a basis for a network, each line of a summary representing either a description of a situation, or a feeling, or a reason. Gradually networks were built to cover as much of the content of the informal summaries as possible. The informal summaries then needed to be recoded so that each contained only terms in the network, making it a formal summary.

Described in outline like this, the process sounds reasonably straightforward, but in fact it was not. Informal summaries constantly produced new items that did not fit into the networks. Networks had to be reshaped or even begun again, and attempts to recode and produce formal summaries had to be ditched until the networks were more effective. Inspection of the networks written at that time would certainly show that they were not very rigourous. In retrospect we feel that their lack of rigour was compensated for by the fact that they allowed us to get some grip on the data.

The final network is too large and complicated to discuss here. Instead, the account will concentrate on some specific aspects of it, chosen to bring out a number of general lessons. The first aspect is the need we found to develop both strategy and content networks. Following that, two parts of the content networks are described: one part which seems reasonably adequate, and a second which presents some reasons for dissatisfaction.

3.1.2 Strategy and Content Networks

When constructing the informal summaries we tried to write these in as natural English as possible. Each new line would begin with a subject and then would say what the subject was doing or was like, for example:

I FELT PLEASED
TEACHER PRAISED ME
SUBJECT IMPORTANT FOR EXAM

A summary would be built out of clauses like these. The clauses would be connected together by links such as WHEN and BECAUSE. We analysed each clause systematically by asking the following two questions:

Who or what is it about?
What sort of thing is being said in the clause?

The first question provided the TOPIC of the clause and the second a COMMENT on it. TOPIC and COMMENT provided the first main distinction in our strategy network, which was then developed further, as follows. Answers to the first question could either be a PERSON - the student himself, the TEACHER or PEERS - or a SITUATION or THING, such as working in a tutorial group or a laboratory.

Many different things could be said in answer to the second question, and were more difficult to deal with. The first most natural division was into two categories: either PROCESSES or STATES OF AFFAIRS, that is, into things which happened, and things which were the case. Thus the student feeling bored and the teacher giving praise are both examples of PROCESSES - the first example being internal and PRIVATE and the latter being external and PUBLIC. By contrast, the teacher being well prepared would count as a STATE OF AFFAIRS. These categories, however, had not yet begun to capture enough detail of what had been said. The nature of the PROCESS varied with the TOPIC as did the STATE OF AFFAIRS. It was, therefore, useful to introduce further features to describe the CHARACTER of the clause, thus qualifying the nature of PROCESSES and STATES OF AFFAIRS.

The first feature, which may or may not be present, is the extent to which a clause has a PERSONAL nature. The teacher giving help in the laboratory and the teacher having a very quiet voice both have a PERSONAL CHARACTER, the first of an INTER-PERSONAL kind, the second of an INDIVIDUAL kind. The second feature we found useful to use was to do with regulating behaviour - with control, influence, or pressure. Thus the marks on a third year project being important for exams could count as an EXTERNAL source of REGULATION whereas the student making a tremendous effort would count as an INTERNAL source of REGULATION.

We needed also to construct a network to describe the LINKS relating clauses. We set up three main distinctions. First, LINKS could be TEMPORAL, describing at what moment the event in a clause occurred in relation to other clauses. Second, a clause could be CAUSAL, such as a student feeling frustrated because the teacher did not mark his work. Lastly a clause could simply be in

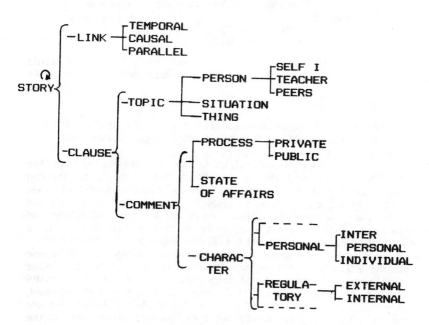

Figure 3.1.1 Strategy network

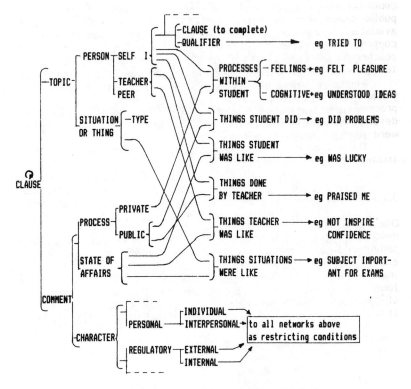

Figure 3.1.2   Clause Network

PARALLEL with other clauses, for example, a student listing a series of reasons why he felt bored with a lecture, with each reason merely coexisting with the others.

Thus a story consists of CLAUSES and LINKS, with any kind of LINK joining any kind of CLAUSE. Recursion is necessary at the beginning of the strategy network so that the chains of LINKS and CLAUSES can each be analysed in turn.

The right hand distinctions drawn out in Figure 3.1.1 now serve as input conditions for a whole series of new networks.

It should be noted that not all the input conditions which can be derived from the strategy network were used, due mainly to the nature of the interview. Thus, because students had been encouraged to talk freely about learning we had some kind of access to the subjective world of what was happening to the student. This permitted us to make the distinction between PUBLIC and PRIVATE PROCESSES, and within PRIVATE PROCESSES we drew another distinction between FEELINGS and COGNITIVE PROCESSES. However, such distinctions could not exist, so far as our data went, for the teacher- where only public things done by the teacher and observed by students were available to us. So when the TEACHER was the topic only two content networks were developed; the first describing what the teacher did (PUBLIC PROCESSES) and the second describing what the teacher was like (STATES OF AFFAIRS).

When the topic input condition was a SITUATION or a THING we found different problems. Teachers and students can carry out processes, but subjects or things cannot. We could only, therefore, develop a content network which described what subjects or things were like for students.

The network in Figure 3.1.2 shows the relationship between the strategy and content networks.

3.1.3 STUDENT/PRIVATE PROCESSES Content Network

One of the central features of the interview was to ask students to describe in some detail how they reacted to the situations they were telling us about. These feelings were extremely wide ranging: from elation to despair, from relief to bewilderment. Figure 3.1.4 (over-leaf) shows the network that we constructed for them, in its complete form. What follows is a simplified, even artificial reconstruction of the process of arriving at the network. The actual process was, of course, much more confused.

A good way to start building the network is just to make a collection of the feelings expressed by students in their interviews. Parts of such a collection would look like this:

1 respect annoyance interest tedium
  fascination waste of time
2 acceptance embarrassment self-confidence
  pride self-doubt inadequacy
3 relief bewilderment anxiety fed-up
  pleasure elation
4 despair achievement frustration defeat
  recognition lack of recognition

These four groups are reflected in Figure 3.1.3.

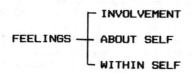

FEELINGS — INVOLVEMENT
         — ABOUT SELF
         — WITHIN SELF

Figure 3.1.3 Main feelings distinctions

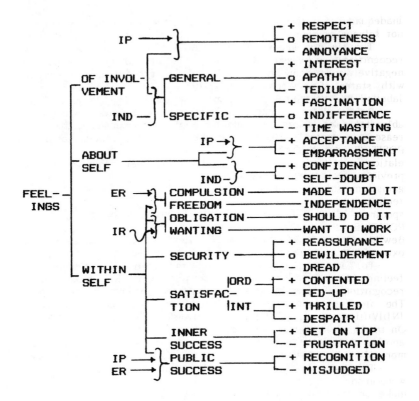

Figure 3.1.4   Network describing students feelings

How did we choose the three main distinctions in Figure 3.1.3 ? Looking at all the feelings in the first block above - from respect to waste of time - we can see that they have to do with some sort of involvement.   Respect and annoyance have respectively to do with POSITIVE and NEGATIVE INVOLVEMENT with the teacher, and are also of an INTERPERSONAL nature.   By contrast interest, tedium, fascination and waste of time express the student's own concern or lack of concern and so are to do with INDIVIDUAL INVOLVEMENT, again NEGATIVE or POSITIVE.

The feelings, in the second block appeared to us to be very different from those discussed above.   They were more about how the student saw himself;   about the image he had of himself as a learner. The INTERPERSONAL and INDIVIDUAL distinction is important here. teacher or peers can influence this image, but no less important is the student on his own being aware that he can or cannot cope with a situation.   Acceptance and embarrassment are clearly feelings that occur when other people are around, whereas self confidence or inadequacy can arise as the result of either being able to solve or not solve a problem.

The feelings in the last two blocks - from relief to lack of recognition - are less easily classified. In a sense we defined them negatively and perhaps inadequately by saying that they were not to do with states of INVOLVEMENT or ideas ABOUT SELF, and were labelled WITHIN SELF.

Despite the problematic nature of this category, within it we were able to make some finer distinctions, which appeared to make reasonable sense. Thus pleasure contrasts with being fed-up as POSITIVE and NEGATIVE kinds of SATISFACTION. So too do elation and despair, but these are rather more intense than the previous pair. Such a grouping is clearly open to doubt. It possibly gains some substance when it is compared with other groupings. Thus feelings of relief, bewilderment and anxiety can all be seen as a spectrum of feelings concerned with SECURITY. Relief expresses POSITIVE SECURITY while anxiety is a feeling of INSECURITY. Bewilderment would seen to come somewhere in between these two extremes as an expression of ABSENCE of SECURITY.

To carry this classification one step further the remaining feelings of achievement, frustration, defeat, recognition and lack of recognition all seem to be an expression of SUCCESS or lack of it. The first three feelings mentioned, however, have more of an INDIVIDUAL nature as do feelings of SECURITY and SATISFACTION. On the other hand recognition or lack of it are much more to do with another person who does or does not acknowledge success, and so have more of an INTERPERSONAL nature.

The categories used in the network were not purely arbitrary, but were in some degree informed by psychological theories. It seemed to make sense to distinguish feelings about self, because of what is known about the importance of self images, and the likelihood that they would be influenced by good or bad incidents. Similarly, many psychologists would expect frustration to be the result of thwarted achievement, so feelings of this kind were placed in the category of NEGATIVE SUCCESS.

3.1.4 TEACHER/STATE OF AFFAIRS Network

The part of the network described here is more problematic. Inevitably teachers were the focus of many of the students' stories, and we wanted to try and capture how students saw them. We introduced as a very first distinction the difference between things that seemed to the student to be the case, and things that could be observed and in principle be objectively agreed upon. This was necessary as some statements about teachers referred to their handwriting, their age, their hair colour or their knowing students' names; visibly recognisable features of the teacher or of his behaviour. By contrast others were more a matter of personal judgment, expressing a view of the teacher's competence or enthusiasm.

Having distinguished between things which SEEMED to be the

case and things that were EXTERNAL, we introduced the input conditions of INDIVIDUAL and INTERPERSONAL. Thus a teacher could seem different when he was on his own, or when he was interacting with students.

Students' comments were also distinguished into those about the teacher's ability or intellectual nature, or his non-academic or more personal, emotional aspects. Thus we distinguished between the COGNITIVE and AFFECTIVE aspects of the teacher. These distinctions gave rise to four groups each of which could describe either the teacher's ACTIONS or the teacher HIMSELF. Figure 3.1.5 shows the complete network for TEACHER/STATE OF AFFAIRS.

Although any one paradigm of this network seemed to provide a reasonable description of the teacher we were less satisfied with the terminals. These had turned into rather too long lists. We should perhaps have attempted either to find meaningful groupings at this level or have rethought the distinctions one level back.

3.1.5 Conclusions

The bulk of the data we were dealing with in this research was daunting - three hundred or so stories, each several pages long. We wanted to be able to retain the characteristics of individual stories, yet be able to compare them.

The development of a strategy network was crucial. Once it was constructed we had a way of organising and analysing the data. Every item of a story in its formal version could be located in the network. The strategy network provided the input conditions necessary to construct the content networks.

The network for students' feelings was developed from the data, but also insights backed by psychological theory were useful in formulating categories at all levels of delicacy.

We were much less happy with the network for the description of teachers, possibly because the interplay between theory and data was less developed. Ideas from psychology as well as from research on teaching styles and management were needed. Weaving all these together to form a sensible framework for categorising was not quite so manageable.

Although a great deal of time and energy was spent developing our networks, we do feel that they permitted us to come to terms with and extract some reasonable results from what otherwise would have remained fascinating but idiosyncratic data.

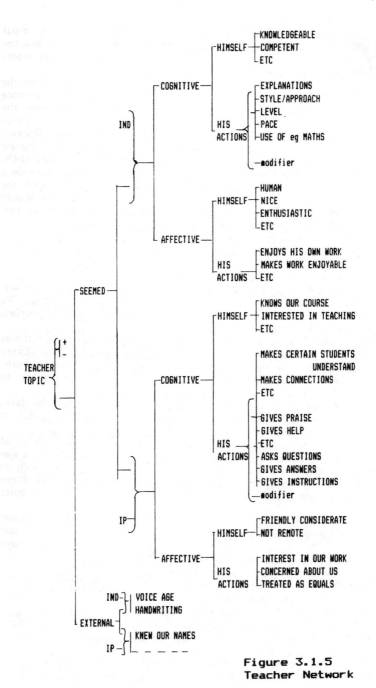

Figure 3.1.5
Teacher Network

3.2 CHILDRENS CLASSIFICATIONS:
USING A NETWORK DEVELOPED BY ANOTHER

by Janet Holland

3.2.1 Introduction

The network which I will discuss here was developed by D. Adlam and B. Bernstein in order to code the responses of eight year old children in an interview which involved them in classifying readily recognisable materials from their everyday life. It was an investigation of children's classification strategies, and the objects for this classification were 24 coloured photographs of food items.(1)
Earlier studies at the Sociological Research Unit, informed by Bernstein's theory of cultural reproduction, suggested that the way in which children talked in different contexts was less a matter of grammar or syntax than of semantics. The children could be said to have differing orientations to meaning. Orientation to meaning can be defined as the selection and organisation of meaning, of what is seen as relevant and taken as the focus of attention in any situation and the ways in which these meanings are organised in practical discourse.
Bernstein argues that the interactional practices of family and school transmit recognition rules which mark contexts as requiring a specific text(2) and realisation rules(3) which regulate what meanings are to be offered and the form in which they should be made public. Families in different social class locations are typified by different interactional practices which regulate different recognition and realisation rules and generate an elaborated or restricted code, or in terms of orientation to meaning, an orientation toward context-independent or context-dependent meanings. Context-dependent meanings centre on aspects of the local and particular situations in which experience of objects, relationships, people and practices are embedded; context-independent meanings tend to separate certain aspects of experience from the situations in which they occur and emphasise the general, transituational features of objects, relationships, people and practices.

3.2.2 The Design of the Study

The study consisted of an extended interview based on a set of 24 colour photographs of food items. Interest was focussed on the types of principles which the children spontaneously and perhaps habitually used to classify familiar materials.
The items (conceptualised exhaustively in terms of a particular set of context-independent principles utilised in part of the interview) were: animal (roast beef, pork chop, sausages, hamburgers, sardines, fish fingers); vegetable (lettuce, green beans, peas, boiled potatoes, chips, baked beans); animal products (milk, butter, cheese, ice-cream, boiled egg, fried egg); and cereal (bread, cakes,

biscuits, rice, rice crispies, spaghetti rings).

The children were interviewed individually for about half an hour and were basically asked questions related to two types of task: (i) they were asked to group the food items and to give reasons for their particular groups;   (ii) the interviewer created various groupings of the items based upon context- independent principles and invited the children to guess her criteria for organising the groups.   Context independent explanations were offered for most of these groups if the child itself had supplied context-dependent criteria.   This section revealed to what extent the child recognised context-independent principles, and provided information and examples of such principles.

The 58 children in the sample were taken from the second year junior classes of four schools in Inner London, selected on the basis of the distribution of parental occupations. Using a broad manual/non manual distinction (4), the schools had children with parents who were either predominantly working class or predominantly middle class.   In the sample the middle class parents were evenly spread in the professions and most working class parents were in the service sector. The distribution of our sample of the basic variables is shown in Table 3.2.1.

GENDER	SOCIAL CLASS GROUP		
	MC	WC	TOTAL
MALE	14	15	29
FEMALE	14	15	29
TOTAL	28	30	58

Table 3.2.1   Gender versus social class

3.2.3   The network used for analysis of the children's responses

The network, Figure 3.2.1, is of the simplest type, a tree diagram, since it makes use of no other notation than the bar.   The terminals are exclusive categories and a paradigm is in effect a terminal.   The major distinction between context-independent and context- dependent meanings appears in two categories which were in fact empirically dominant, GENERAL PRINCIPLES and EVERYDAY USE.

3.2.4   The Original Conceptualisation of the Network: Definitions

The main two theory-based categories of the network are CONTEXT INDEPENDENT and CONTEXT DEPENDENT.   Each category and its further levels of delicacy will be described in turn.

GENERAL PRINCIPLES is the basic CONTEXT INDEPENDENT category in which the children's contextualisations (5) refer to the transituational properties of the items. It is the category most akin to logical classification for which there is a hierarchical taxonomy. This category is described in greater detail through the following three subcategories:

> TRANSFORMATION: here the child makes reference to the fact that one or more items in the group is made from another item in the group, or that all items in the group are made from similar ingredients. Examples are milk or butter - 'butter is made from milk' (non-exhaustive), or chips or boiled potatoes - 'chips are made out of potatoes' (exhaustive).
> GENERIC and ORIGIN: The generic category can be thought of in contrast to that of origin. In the first case the child's rationale includes a common category name, for instance, meat, fish, eggs, vegetables, whereas to be included under the heading 'origin' the rationale must make explicit reference to where the items come from. Thus roast beef, sausages, pork chop - 'all comes from animals' (non- exhaustive).

The exhaustive/non-exhaustive distinction is presented in the network as at a greater level of delicacy, but is in fact at the same level as the main subcategories in the CONTEXT INDEPENDENT, GENERAL PRINCIPLES category, and is supplementary to them.

The four categories which make up the CONTEXT DEPENDENT category are FOOD ATTRIBUTES, PERCEPTUAL FEATURES, AMBIGUOUS/IMPLICIT and EVERYDAY USE. Each of these categories and its subcategories are now described in order to get a clearer picture of CONTEXT DEPENDENT meanings.

In the category of FOOD ATTRIBUTES the child refers to particular features which food items have in common, as follows:

> TASTE, but excluding nice and nasty which are personal preferences and are included in the EVERYDAY USE category.
> TEXTURE, for example, fish fingers, rice crispies - 'they're both crunchy'.
> EFFECTS, relates to consequences of eating particular foods, for example, bread, cakes, chips, rice, ice-cream, - 'these things are fattening'.
> PREPARATION, makes reference to cooking methods or means of storage.

In the PERCEPTUAL FEATURES category the child refers to visually apparent properties of the items depicted in the picture such as colour and shape, or to the words used to describe the item which was included on the stimulus material.

An AMBIGUOUS/IMPLICIT category was necessary as it is possible for a child to group a number of cards together and talk about this group without being able to recover the basis on which the items were categorised. For example, if a child put together baked beans and boiled potatoes and tells us that 'they go together' we cannot be sure whether this grouping is based on the use of the items (e.g. that they may be eaten together) or on perceptual features (e.g. that all these items are round in shape). There are three sub-categories of the AMBIGUOUS/IMPLICIT CATEGORY:

DESCRIPTIVE: the child merely describes the set.
ASSOCIATIVE: the child says the items go together without explaining why this is so.
SIMILAR/DIFFERENT: the child says a group of items are alike, or on rare occasions that they are different, but does not go on to say on what basis this is so.

The EVERDAY USE category is the basic CONTEXT DEPENDENT category where the children contextualise the items in terms of their everyday experience of the practical use of food. This category is

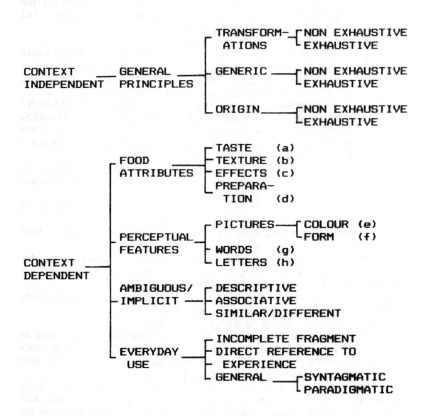

Figure 3.2.1 Network used initially

described in greater detail through the following three subcategories:

INCOMPLETE FRAGMENT: this form of rationale was rare in the data but is distinct from the other headings in this sub-category. The child clearly is making reference to practical use but does not embed this linguistically in a form which specifies to whom the practice refers. Examples are rice crispies, milk - 'in the morning', baked beans, bread - 'lunch'.

DIRECT REFERENCE TO EXPERIENCE: rationales which refer directly to a child's own experience are coded in this sub-category. A child may refer to herself or mention particular family members or friends, and personal likes and dislikes are also included here. Examples include fried eggs, chips - 'Mummy sometimes makes it like that', roast beef, peas, boiled potatoes - 'that's what we have for Sunday dinner.'

GENERAL: described at a greater level of delicacy by the following two sub-categories:

GENERAL SYNTAGMATIC: here the child makes a more general statement about foods that are typically eaten together. Many of the statements coded in this category include the personal pronoun 'you' and the referrent of this pronoun is often difficult to specify. It may refer to a particular 'you', perhaps the addressee, or more likely the referrent may be 'you in general' which is synonymous with the English 'one'. For example, cakes, biscuits, milk - 'you have these together', sausages, baked beans - 'you can have sausages and baked beans for tea'.

GENERAL PARADIGMATIC: examples in this category refer explicitly to one particular meal, the items forming a list of options from a possible menu. For example, fish fingers, hamburgers, sausages, baked beans, spaghetti rings, fried eggs, chips, bread and butter.

3.2.5 Problems in Taking Over an Analysis

At the time when I took over the analysis of data on this project, the children's responses on their own first two sortings of the food items had already been analysed. My problem had several components. First, the coding frame which had been generated to capture the children's contextualisations for their own sortings, already analysed, was obviously appropriate for their third sorting, an exactly similar task. The only problem here was coder reliability, and in this connection the solution was to work through all the coding undertaken by my predecessor to familiarise myself entirely with her under-standing of the categories. Secondly, was the network which had been developed to analyse and code the children's relatively spontaneous sorting activity appropriate to deal with the recognition tasks in the interview? In this case I decided to revert to the basic theoretical distinction between context-dependent and context- independent responses, but implicitly using the categories of the more elaborated network in order to allocate responses into these more general categories.

Thirdly, did I in fact agree with the coding categories and their ability to capture the meanings the children were using in their responses? Here I did rework two sections of the network to look at this problem. Finally, did I consider the underlying theoretical distinction between context-independent and context-dependent principles adequate and appropriate for use with this data? Here my problems were related to (a) the nature of the distinction itself and its relation to formal classification, and (b) the specific items which were used as stimulus materials. The last two points are discussed in the next section.

3.2.6 A Reformulation of Parts of the Network

In my view some of the context-dependent categories in the network generated principles which could produce logical classes and which could refer to general, transituational properties of the stimulus items, that is, be more appropriately classified as context-independent in terms of the basic dichotomy. It was possible that a reworking from this point of view might lead to changes in the relative position of our two social class groups in terms of use of context-independent and context-dependent meanings. The two sections for which I considered this change were food attributes and perceptual principles.

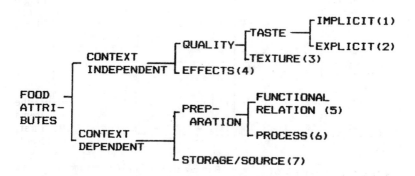

Figure 3.2.2 Food attributes revised network

49

The part of the revised network for food attributes is shown in Figure 3.2.2. The categories of taste (excluding personal likes and dislikes), texture, and effects of eating various types of food are now seen as abstractions from the stimulus items, drawing attention to principles for organising the material which go beyond everyday experience although based upon it, and which are conceivably capable of generating an exhaustive taxonomy. Methods of preparation are seen as more closely related to the everyday experience of food, as are means of storage or references to shops where such food is obtainable.

Table 3.2.2 gives changes resulting from this recoding. This table should be viewed in the light of the overall results of the study, where middle class children are more likely than working class children (a) to use context-independent (original definition) contextualisations; and (b) when using such responses to give half or more of their own total responses in that section of the interview in

	ORIGINAL CODING					NEW CODING								
	CONTEXT DEPENDENT RESPONSES					CONTEXT IND. RESPONSES					CONTEXT DEP. RESPONSES			
	a	b	c	d	S	1	2	3	4	S	5	6	7	S
FIRST CLAS-SIFICATION MC	10	2	1	8	15	0	10	2	1	12	3	5	0	7
WC	2	1	1	4	7	1	1	1	1	4	0	2	2	4
SECOND CLAS-SIFICATION MC	6	2	0	6	12	1	6	1	0	8	0	5	1	6
WC	0	0	2	3	5	0	0	2	0	2	0	3	0	5
THIRD CLAS-SIFICATION MC	9	0	1	12	18	0	9	0	1	10	3	10	1	12
WC	8	1	2	3	11	5	3	2	1	10	2	2	0	4

KEY

a to d refer to Figure 3.2.1
1 to 7 refer to Figure 3.2.2

S is the number of children responding
(Note that a child can give responses in more than one sub-category)

Table 3.2.2 Old and new coding compared
for food attributes

the context-independent category. The exception to this general pattern in the overall study is the child's second classification, where working class children continue to give largely context dependent responses, and a number of middle class children who had initially given context-independent contextualisations, switch into context-dependent responses.

We can see from Table 3.2.2 that for the recoding, contrary to the main study, more working class children use context-independent attribute contextualisations on their third classification than they did in their previous classifications, whereas more middle class children use context-dependent attribute contextualisations.

In the case of perceptual features it seemed that the children who abstracted colour, size and form from the photographic representations of the stimulus items might be using principles for organising the materials drawn from other sorting tasks where more abstract materials might be used. Once again these criteria could conceivably generate logical classes of items in the set and could be seen as abstractions from the specific context of the stimulus card and depicted items. On the other hand, reference to the descriptive words on the cards, or letters in them, seemed very context bound. See Figure 3.2.3.

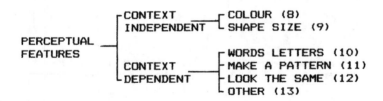

Figure 3.2.3 Perceptual features revised network

Table 3.2.3 gives the results from this revision of the network. Once again we uncover a greater use of context- independent responses, especially in the third classification on the part of the working class children than was the case with the original network, where all perceptual responses were regarded as context-dependent. In terms of the analysis undertaken on this data and presented at the most general level in Holland (1981) no difference is made in the overall results by these changes. But they do indicate that slight alterations in the definition of the context-independent, context-dependent categories, does make a difference to the results of the two social class groups at a more delicate level, and especially for the working class group, in terms of their use of context-independent meanings in their own productions.

| | ORIGINAL CODING | | | | | NEW CODING | | | | | | | |
| | CONTEXT DEP. RESPONSES | | | | | CONTEXT IND. RESPONSES | | | CONTEXT DEPENDENT RESPONSES | | | | |
	e	f	g	h	S	8	9	S	10	11	12	13	S
FIRST CLAS-SIFICATION MC	2	2	0	0	4	1	1	2	0	0	1	1	2
WC	3	2	0	0	4	3	2	3	1	0	0	0	1
SECOND CLAS-SIFICATION MC	1	3	1	2	7	0	3	3	2	0	2	1	4
WC	1	1	0	0	2	1	0	1	0	1	0	0	1
THIRD CLAS-SIFICATION MC	1	3	1	0	7	1	3	4	1	0	0	0	1
WC	7	1	1	1	7	7	1	7	1	0	0	0	1

KEY

e to h refer to Figure 3.2.1   S is the number of children responding
8 to 13 refer to Figure 3.2.3   (Note that a child can give responses in
more than one sub-category)

**Table 3.2.3   Old and new coding compared
for perceptual features**

3.2.7   Concluding Comments

One could argue that true classification in the sense of the joint application of the logical definition of classification by intension (specifying the properties shared by class members) and extension (listing members of the class) is more applicable to the case where context-independent general principles are employed, and that context-dependent principles do not generate logical classes.   As we have seen above, however, this neat mapping of the context-independent/dependent dichotomy onto a definition of logical classification is not as easy as it may seem, despite the fact that in the specific instance of the stimulus items used here, an hierarchical taxonomy of categories of food is readily available.   Some of the categories defined as context dependent can generate logical classes.

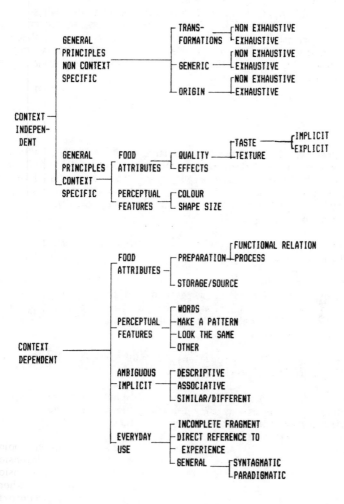

Figure 3.2.4   Possible revised network
               incorporating discussed changes

A further question is raised by the potential issue of the use of 'collections' rather than 'classes' (Markman and Seibert 1976, Carbonnel 1978). If the items in this set of stimulus materials had been more readily amenable to such organisation into 'collections', would we have seen this option being taken up by each of our social class groups, or would the clear differences between them which were observed in the main part of the study reported here be maintained? The recategorisation carried out and just described with 'classes' would suggest that the matter is open to empirical test that might benefit from the careful reorganisation of theoretical categories that network notation allows.

Notes:

(1) The results of the study are written up in Holland J., 'Social Class and Changes in Orientation to Meaning', Sociology, Vol. 15, No 1, February 1981, and in considerably more detail in a mimeo report SRU/SSRC 5, by Adlam, D and Holland,, J., 'Classification strategies employed by eight year old children: a study of difference in orientation to meaning'.

(2) A text is the linguistic production and includes both semantic and lexical/grammatical choices.

(3) For further explication of the terms recognition and realisation rules, previously referred to as ground and performance rules in Bernstein's work, see 'Codes, Modalities and the Process of Cultural Reproduction: A Model', Pedagogical Bulletin, 7, Department of Education, University of Lund, Sweden, 1980.

(4) See Office of Population Censuses and Surveys, Classification of Occupations 1970, London, HMSO, 1970.

(5) We use this term for the children's rationales for their groups since it is by telling us why they think a group of items go together that they give us access to the context through which they have accorded meaning to the set of items in question.

3.3 PERCEPTIONS OF PUPILS' PERFORMANCE

by Tony Orgee

3.3.1 The Study

This paper should be seen in the context of the debate about standards of pupil performance, a debate which can be conducted in terms of whether standards are rising or falling, requiring evidence about performance over time, or of whether standards are high enough, needing data for just one time as the basis for discussion. The following research is located in terms of the second type of discussion.

As part of its accountability initiative the Social Science Research Council funded a project based at Chelsea College which looked closely at the issue of standards and pupil performance in science. The project was part philosophical and part empirical. The empirical work used items from the science monitoring programme of the Assessment of Performance Unit as the basis for exploring perceptions of pupil performance. The views of various groups whom it was thought might be interested in APU results when they were eventually published were sought. Primary and secondary teachers, science educators, local authority advisers, parents and employers were all involved in the work. Interest centred on the range of views put forward, and on the variation in views both between and within groups.

In the pilot phase of the empirical work individual interviews were conducted with teachers and parents. Each interview focussed on a small number of separate APU items, the number depending on the time available. Prior to any discussion the respondent wrote down his or her own answers to all the items and then examined the mark schemes. The intention was to gain insight into the expectations of performance (not how pupils would perform but rather how pupils ought to perform) held by different groups, with a view to relating these expectations to actual results when these emerged. The interviews sought to ascertain what was the lowest level of pupil performance on the items which respondents would consider acceptable, indeed to see if such levels existed and the reasons for any such expectation. In practice the respondents wanted to talk about the problems and the difficulties they had with the items and mark scheme. Many went on to consider how they thought pupils would actually perform on the items before addressing the issue of the lowest acceptable level of performance. Further examination of the pilot data revealed not only a wide variety of opinion on current levels of performance, but also considerable diversity in the reasons advanced for such predictions. It was apparent that the basis on which respondents replied varied considerably from one to another. Issues raised by one respondent seemed to be either completely ignored or tacitly assumed by others.

The results of the pilot work suggested that the main study should have a double thrust: a small collection of open-ended interviews in order to explore more fully the diversity of responses and an open-ended questionnaire sent out to a larger number of people to supplement the interviews. The agenda for the interview and questionnaire would be the same: the questionnaire would, however, contain rating scales for ease-difficulty and for importance of APU items. The respondent was asked to:

1. Answer the item.
2. Explain why he did not score full marks (interview only).
3. Predict the actual pupil performance level on that item.
4. State the lowest level of performance he would consider as acceptable.
5. React to two sets of hypothetical performance data for the item.

The net result of this work was a mass of complex and wide ranging data from several hundred respondents. To do justice to the data it had to be reported in such a way as to bring out its complexity and scope, while simultaneously distinguishing the essence from the fine detail. Networks offered one possible solution.

The main concern of this paper is to outline the development of a network to cope with the prediction of pupil performance level on APU items, the reasons for the predictions, and a rating of the ease of an item. As will be seen this turned out to be somewhat more complicated than was initially anticipated.

3.3.2 Developing a Network

In attempting to draw up the network in Figure 3.3.1 the following issues were considered:

If respondents predict a level of pupil performance on a given item, what is the level, what are the reasons for this level and what is the ease/difficulty rating of the item?

If respondents cannot predict a level, what are their reasons?

Such a scheme is shown in Figure 3.3.1. It may seem to be no more than commonsense, yet unfortunately it does not describe the data. A more accurate description of responses is given in Figure 3.3.2.

The network notation in Figure 3.3.2 is able to convey immediately interesting and perhaps surprising information. Some respondents made a prediction but were not able to say how easy or difficult an item would be for an 11 year old; others were able to explain why they could not give a prediction and yet went on to rate the item. There were, of course, those who gave prediction and rating and those who gave neither.

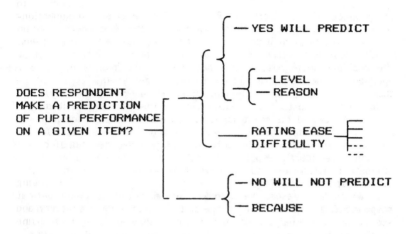

Figure 3.3.1   First attempt at network for
              APU items

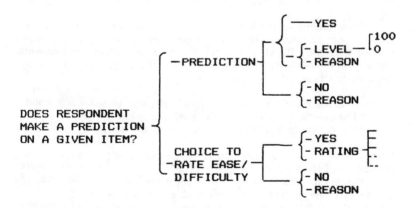

Figure 3.3.2   Revised version of network
               in Figure 3.3.1

3.3.3 Expanding Part of the Network (Reasons for Predictions)

To produce the network in Figure 3.3.2 required no more than technique, combing the data for all the possible combinations. The hard work began when it came to constructing that part of the network which dealt with respondents' reasons for their predictions. Part of the problem arose out of the fact that in the main study a fairly open-ended questionnaire had been used to get at this aspect of the task and that quite often the meanings were a little vague. However it was possible to take any reason and see that it could be considered from a number of different aspects. Three of these aspects, that is, what the focus of the reason was, its scope and the basis for the reason, were fairly easily defined and will be described in this section. A fourth aspect, the nature of the reason, presented a number of difficulties and these will be discussed further in Section 3.3.4.

When the reasons were looked at in detail it was seen that respondents gave a minimum of one or two reasons up to a maximum of six reasons. Analysis of the reasons showed that each had a particular focus or subject. Four main foci emerged according to which the reasons could initially be classified. These were: the form of the APU item, the children themselves, the teaching, and the performance of others. There were also a number of reasons that had no real focus but that were, in fact, in a tautological category. Thus a respondent who predicted that about 50% of pupils would succeed gave as a reason for this that, "Just over half of them will answer correctly".

When looked at more closely each of the sub-categories of the focus aspect could be defined in greater detail. For example, where the form of the APU item was the focus of the reason, respondents' replies very clearly referred to different features. Listed below are some of the types of response given:

"It is not clear what the question wants you to do".
"The question requires a high level of reading skills".
"The concepts involved in the question are difficult".

These responses can be described as centred on item presentation, item demands and item content respectively.

Turning now to the other two aspects mentioned earlier, the first of these, scope, refers to the level of generality of the reason. So, to say that 'children do not read questions carefully', is to make a general point about how children answer written items and does not refer to the specific APU item under consideration. When it came to considering the basis for a reason it could be seen that respondents' reasons referred either to their beliefs or their knowledge. Thus the following two comments can be seen to be based on different premises:

"I don't know whether this is taught in primary schools or not. I don't think (believe) it is".
"I know this is generally taught".

These three aspects are now introduced into the network in Figure 3.3.3 which develops the part of the network described in Figure 3.3.2 concerned with reasons for predictions.

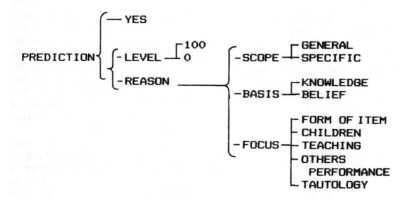

Figure 3.3.3   Development of network
in Figure 3.3.2

3.3.4   Difficulties with the Expansion of the Network

Although the aspects of SCOPE, BASIS and FOCUS, shown in Figure 3.3.3 seemed to go some way in characterising the reasons given by the respondents it did seem as though more could be said about them. The nature of each reason as a whole could be described. When the reasons were analysed in this manner it was seen that each made some attempt to explain why an item could be successfully answered or not. In a sense it could be said that the nature of the reason had a negative or positive polarity. In considering how to cope with this problem there seemed to be two possible ways of proceeding. A first would be to take each of the sub-categories of the FOCUS aspect, in turn, and attempt to define them at a further level of delicacy. A second way would be to consider the nature of the reason and its polarity at the same level as the other three aspects and attempt to find a more general decription for them.

Both of the above ways have been attempted, but neither has yet reached a satisfactory conclusion. In turning to the first approach, the sub-category of CHILDREN under the FOCUS aspect was looked at more closely. On examination it can be seen that respondents talked about children's experiences and abilities, how they thought children would approach the items and what they thought children's attitudes would be to the given item. Some examples of these reasons follow.

"Children are taught this". (Experience)
"Most children have the ability to understand the question".
 (Ability)
"Children do not read questions carefully". (Approach)
"Children find graphs boring". (Attitude).

These examples can also be categorised according to whether they are expressed in a positive or negative way.
Taking this attempt to define further the sub-category of CHILDREN, together with the sub-category of FORM OF ITEM already discussed in Section 3.2.3 the beginnings of a network to show the further levels of delicacy of the FOCUS aspect would look something like the one outlined in Figure 3.3.4.

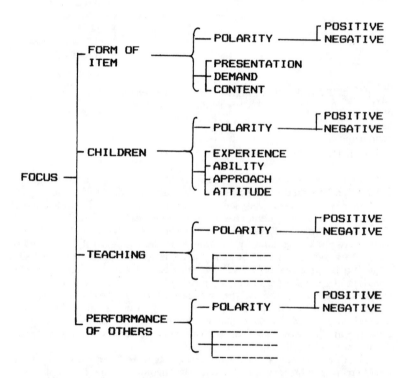

Figure 3.3.4 Further levels of delicacy of FOCUS

The network in Figure 3.3.4 seemed to indicate from its far right-hand distinctions that the feature of POSITIVE/NEGATIVE POLARITY was a more global aspect of the reason due to its constant repetition. This consideration led to taking the second approach mentioned previously, and so the responses were looked at afresh in order to find a more general way of describing them.

Looking at the following examples, it can be seen that some reasons suggested why an item could be successfully attempted:

(1) "It is straight-forward and clear".
(2) "They are taught this".
(3) "The question is easy to understand".
(4) "Pupils enjoy..."

Other reasons attempted to explain why an item would be answered incorrectly:

(5) "Some do not make an effort"
(6) "A few will not have the ability to understand what is required".

Clearly a distinction simply recording the polarity of the reason did not capture sufficiently what the respondents were attempting to say; the difficulty itself needed to be characterised in some way in order to get a complete description. In Figure 3.3.5 a first attempt has been made to incorporate these ideas into the part of the network concerned with reasons for predictions.

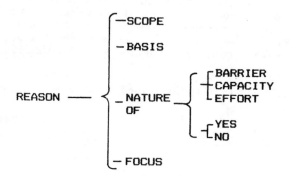

Figure 3.3.5 Further levels of delicacy
NATURE OF question

The network designation of reasons (1) to (6) would then have been (with SCOPE and BASIS not coded) as follows:

(1)	BARRIER NO QUESTION
(2)	BARRIER NO TEACHING
(3)	BARRIER NO QUESTION
(4)	EFFORT YES CHILDREN
(5)	EFFORT NO CHILDREN
(6)	CAPACITY NO CHILDREN

It was thought, however, that these codings were not very reliable as alternatively good ones could be given from the network. Perhaps reason (6) best illustrates this problem as 'the lack of understanding' referred to in the reason could also be interpreted as a barrier to coping with the item and so the coding could read (6) BARRIER YES CHILDREN. Thus while the distinctions BARRIER/ CAPACITY/EFFORT attempt to capture a very real facet of the nature of the reason and its polarity they do not manage to do it unambiguously. Work is, however, continuing in this area as the author believes that it is important for the network to reflect the nature of the response at this level.

3.3.5 Conclusion

The network discussed above is just one aspect of the work presently being carried out. Networks are also being developed to describe on the one hand reasons for deciding on lowest acceptable levels of performance, and on the other reactions to sets of hypothetical data. This will eventually lead to the production of a 'telegram' for each individual respondent for each APU item they considered. It is hoped that such a format will allow 'telegrams' of individuals to be compared and thus similarities and differences between people in groups and between groups to be drawn out and compared.

ACKNOWLEDGEMENT: all items used in this work by permission of the D.E.S.

USING NETWORKS TO REPRESENT
KAREN'S KNOWLEDGE OF MATHS

by Nancy Johnson

3.4.1   Introduction

I used a network as one way of representing a part of the mathematical
knowledge of one child.   That knowledge was embedded in several semi-
structured interviews with a 12 year old girl - Karen.   The subject
was 'SUMS'.   Karen was one of eight children who had been interviewed
and network analysis was one of several forms of representation used
in   the   general   methodological   study   -   problems   of   eliciting   and
reporting mathematical knowledge in school children.   Two versions of
a network will be discussed.   I shall describe some of the ideas I was
trying to encapsulate in the network, and say why the second version
is an improvement on the first.

      Although a novice to writing networks, I did not come unarmed to
the task!   I   had a synopsis of Karen's interview transcripts and
fairly definite ideas about the kind of network I wanted.   Primarily
it must reflect the quality of Karen's knowledge and so might be
highly   idiosyncratic.

      It certainly should not be a network of mathematical structure
such as Figure 3.4.1 (a) since Karen's experience of mathematics had
not encompassed anything as sophisticated as varieties of algebraic
structure or different kinds of mathematical activity.   Neither could
I   write   a   'pedagogic'   network   like   Figure   3.4.1   (b)   which   split
mathematics   into   ideas   and   techniques   involving   topics   like   place
value, associative operation and the other notions well beloved of
mathematics teachers.   Yet I knew more than the feeble demoralised
version of Figure 3.4.1 (c).

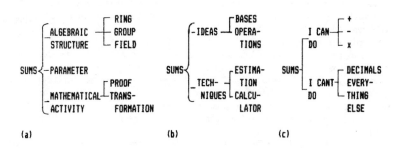

(a)   (b)   (c)

Figure 3.4.1   Different unacceptable
representations of Karen's knowledge

3.4.2   The First Network

What seemed to be obvious to Karen was firstly that there are different kinds of sums. Often each has two names, one deriving from primary school and another 'received'. Great importance is attached to the layout of these sums. Secondly sums have characteristic elements, like number, signs, answer. And lastly, sums are 'what you do', and there are several different kinds of 'things to do', for instance, destroying brackets in Simplifying Sums or drawing Venn diagrams in Set Sums.

This produces a set of three loose categories: sums, their various names and appearances; sums, their constituents; and sums, as various actions; which seemed to be a reasonable basis for a schematic network. I could start on the left hand side with:

VARIETY of sum (by name and picture)
OBJECTS (the constituents of sums-signs, answers, numbers)
INSTRUCTION TO DO (of which there are varieties)

and somewhere in the dim blue haze of the right-hand side would be the more delicate terms:

times
multiplication
+ - x (signs)
add, then carry

Figure 3.4.2 shows my first attempt to write the network given in Figure 3.4.4.

The extra term SETTING was introduced to reflect the idea that Karen would assign most sums to either the joint group ARITH-METIC/ALGEBRA (later called ARAL) or SETS.

Even in this primitive version it is apparent that there will be several nodes with the same name appearing in different parts of the network. A cursory glance at the network in Figure 3.4.4 reveals that the terms VARIETY and NAME each appear three times. This kind of repetition occurred partly as a throwback to another approach to representing Karen's knowledge where Variety and Name were key distinctions. Networks appeared to be good at revealing mental barnacles! But there was another, more positive, reason for repeating terms, which was related to the overall purpose of the network. I wanted to be able to generate pieces of extended code which would each be a description of a type of sum in Karen's repertoire e.g. fractions or long division.

During the interviews, the child tried to teach me her point of view. The dialogue would continue until the child was satisfied that I had learned what she herself knew. My notes made on paper and my post-interview summaries were inspected by the child, to test if I had hold of the right end of the arithmetic stick. (All of the data collection was completed before I had any useful knowledge of network

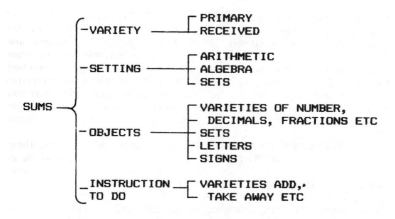

Figure 3.4.2   Initial outline of first version
given in Figure 3.4.4

analysis so Karen never saw a network.)   In order to remain faithful
to Karen's ideas, I chose to construct the network in such a way that
the codes would read as descriptions of sums which would (perhaps
paraphrased) be acceptable to Karen herself.

The idea of building up the network so that it appeared to operate
from left to right (or at least should be read from left to right)
emerged as a key idea at this point.   It dominated all subsequent work
on the first version, Figure 3.4.4, and endured as the characteristic
feature of the second version, Figure 3.4.5.

The next step was to attempt a small section in detail.   Karen's
transcript gave three immediate features which I wanted to incorporate
in the network.

1. There are several varieties of signs.
2. Each variety is a signal for an action.   (I created a node
    ACTIVATOR   to   reflect   this   signalling/instructional
    quality).
3. The appearance of the sum on the page was distinctive and
    in need of description.   Karen could identify the approp-
    priate answer-finding procedure by the choice of the format
    on the page.   The type and position of the sign was impor-
    tant to her.   (For this point I used two nodes: DISPLAY
    meaning the picture of the sign on the page; SYNTAX
    meaning the context.)

Figure 3.4.3 shows how these three points were developed in a
small part of the network.

When I turned my attention to the ACTIVATOR node, I found
myself writing a large chunk of arithmetic procedures, which properly

belonged under the node 'INSTRUCTION TO DO'. Subsuming arithmetic procedures under OBJECTS was more than just an awkwardness of the formalism; it was conceptually absurd. My 'solution' was to leave the ACTIVATOR node undeveloped but marked as a bad area. It was already clear that I needed a new design altogether! However I continued. I concentrated on creating nodes which reflected relevant features of Karen's knowledge, and tried to arrange them so as to generate sentence-like codes. I was trying to code SUM types in this way:

SUM (VARIETY (NAME (INTEGERS; DISPLAY   3+(-4) =
SETTING (ALGEBRA; etc.   -4+(+3) =

and was not interested in looking at the terminals alone.

The rest of the network (Figure 3.4.4, page 68) was developed with an eye to the left-right unfolding of the code and not with any regard to the possible combinations of terminal elements. Although most combinations make sense there are several which do not, for example,

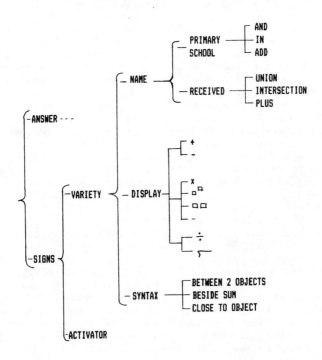

Figure 3.4.3   Development of small section of network in FIGURE 3.4.4

```
VARIETY   (NAME   (Long Multiplication)
OBJECTS (constituents (sets))
```

is illegal for Karen, since she would never attempt to do long multiplication with sets.

A typical across-the-page code for Long Multiplication was now:

```
VARIETY    (NAME (ORDINARY SUM (LONG MULTIPLICATION)))
           (DISPLAY (set out in rows))
SETTING    (ARITHMETIC)
OBJECTS    (CONSTITUENTS (NUMBERS (WHOLE (ORDINARY)
                                    DECIMALS)))
           (SYNTAX (SIGNS (VARIETY (NAME
                           (PRIMARY SCHOOL (TIMES))
                           RECEIVED (MULTIPLICATION)
                           DISPLAY (X)
                           SYNTAX (BESIDE SUM)))
INSTRUCTIONS TO DO
           (VARIETY (NAME (PRIMARY SCHOOL (NONE)
                           RECEIVED (MULTIPLYING))
                    ACTION (STEPWISE (VARIETY
                    (WORK OUT SUM (ARITHMETIC))))))
```

This is paraphrasable as:

"The name of this sum is long multiplication. It is an ordinary sum in arithmetic with this format. It is done with decimals and whole numbers. Another name for it is times and the answer goes below the sum. You work out the sum in steps using arithmetic."

The ARITHMETIC node was undeveloped for the time being. That was a symptom of my problem with the ACTIVATOR node.

3.4.3 A Revised Network

The major revisions in ·the second version, Figure 3.4.5 were as follows. First, the SETTING and NAME (stored in two places in the network in Figure 3.4.4) were conflated into one node. This was done because Karen   identified her sums by name rather than setting.   This new node NAME carried the concept of variety of sum and of action.   In a sense, Karen selected a name and the appropriate procedure followed automatically and so, I reasoned, the notion of variety of sum really belonged with names rather than actions.   VARIETY now only appeared once in the whole network - a rather more elegant appearance than the first attempt.

Also, the INSTRUCTION TO DO node was rewritten according to the character of the action performed. This could be an action performed on the objects on the page, for example, standard arithmetic, or it could be an action where you needed to employ another idea, for example, the number line or drawing a pie chart.

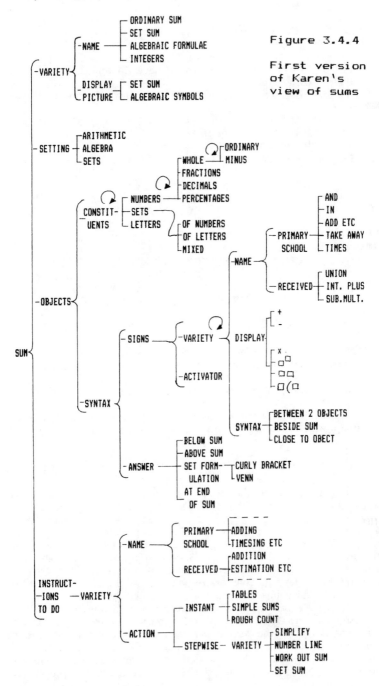

Figure 3.4.4

First version
of Karen's
view of sums

Figure 3.4.5

Second version
of Karen's
view of sums

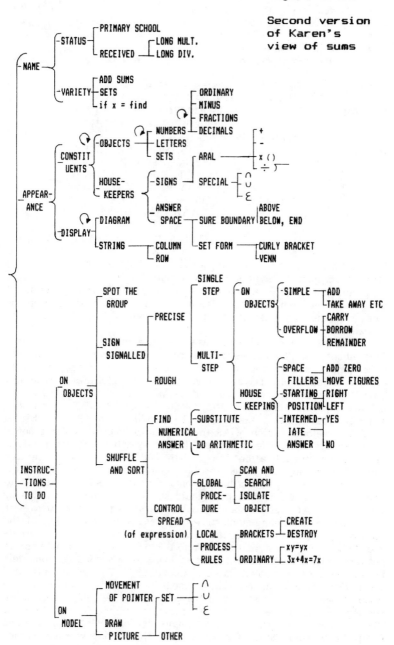

69

Lastly, the ON OBJECTS node is more developed because Karen talked much more about that kind of action. She was just beginning to learn about generalised number and all the other baggage of algebra and it gave me an opportunity to try and capture very fragile and half learned ideas.

With these changes, Long Multiplication now coded up as follows:

```
NAME          (STATUS (PRIMARY SCHOOL)
                VARIETY (LONG MULTIPLICATION))
APPEARANCE (CONSTITUENTS (OBJECTS (NUMBERS
                            (ORDINARY) DECIMALS))
              DISPLAY (STRING (COLUMN)))
INSTRUCTIONS TO DO (ON OBJECTS (SIGN SIGNALLED
                        (PRECISE (MULTISTEP
                        (ON OBJECTS (SIMPLE (TIMES)
                        (OVERFLOW (CARRY))
              HOUSEKEEPING (SPACE FILLERS
                        (ADD ZEROES)
                        START (LEFT)
                        INTERMEDIATE ANSWER (YES))))
```

This says much the same as the previous coding except that the code stopped abruptly at arithmetic. Now added is the information that long multiplication is a precise, sign signalled, multistep string of actions on the numerical objects, and furthermore, that to keep the sum in shape you must start on the left and fill in the gaps with zeros.

Looking at the network now as a one-page display of Karen's global ideas about sums, the names of nodes refer to concepts that I had when developing it and are not immediately perspicuous to a reader. Some of the terms in my private language had the following meanings. SIGNS are still a constituent of SUMS, but INSTRUCTIONS TO DO are now signalled by SIGNS, OPERATE ON OBJECTS, and need some HOUSEKEEPING features. The curious term ARAL in Figure 3.4.5 is a welded version of ARithmetic and ALgebra. Karen grouped together the signs like + - x and brackets with the syntactic form of denoting multiplication (3b = 3xb, and indices) and separated this ARAL group from other special signs used in Set Sums (∩∪{}). It is not surprising that, having only recently been introduced to 'sums with X's and Y's', Karen should see them as near relatives of arithmetic. At present she has only a first acquaintance with sets.

I admit to feeling much more confident about the ability of the second version to encapsulate interesting features of Karen's knowledge. The first version looked as clumsy as a first attempt at network writing might be expected to look. The second version felt better because it looked more economical. The gross left-hand distinctions of Sum name, what it looks like and the type of action involved were major distinctions made by Karen herself. The action section, in particular, was more developed in the second version. Whereas the first version had a simple list of varieties of actions (simplify, number line, work out sum...), the second version characterised those same actions by features (precise, rough, simple, overflow, control spread ...).

The network also shows (by omission) that there are certain gaps in Karen's knowledge. There is no connection between arithmetic operations. Multiplication is not linked to addition nor division to subtraction. Set Sums (intersections and unions) are just another kind of sum. They are not seen to be part of algebra.

The network also shows what she does know. Although arithmetic and algebraic signs form a group called ARAL, there is a definite change in character between arithmetic and algebraic procedures. Algebra for Karen is more than just arithmetic where someone is hiding the true identity of the 'unknown' - an idea commonly found in children learning about algebra. Had Karen been a victim to this particular misconception, the shuffle and sort node would have been a lesser distinction made at the level of simple overflow actions on objects. As it is, she has an idea that there is another large category of sum; hence, the shuffle and sort node emerges as a greater left hand distinction.

3.4.4   Conclusions

Inevitably Karen's knowledge was incomplete or ill-defined in places. It could hardly be otherwise for anyone engaged in learning a complex subject. In fact she was a clever 12-year old who had obviously been paying attention in class. To be able to write any description of this precarious knowledge, embedded in 70 pages of transcript, seemed like quite a task. The aim had been to see if a network, a well-defined system, could cope with the ill-defined character of Karen's knowledge. To have been able to produce Figure 3.4.5 at all indicates that the exercise was successful to some degree!

The actual process of constructing the network was also an aid in getting to know my data. The network revealed that there was structure in Karen's world of mathematics that had not been obvious in other attempts at representing her knowledge (e.g. characteristics of actions). Through the discipline of network writing, I gained a vocabulary for communicating what I knew about Karen - a major aim of the overall study. To be able to present a graphical summary on one sheet of paper was an added bonus.

3.5 A NETWORK DESCRIPTION OF COMMENTS ON PEERS

by Martin Monk

3.5.1 Introduction

In this example I want to discuss the use of networks as an aid to handling large numbers of free responses to an open questionnaire. Free response data of this type has many of the benefits of qualitative data gathered by more costly means such as interviews. At the same time if a method can be found for codifying the responses the data can become amenable to statistical analysis. Networks prove to be a very useful tool for this purpose.

What is reported here is just a small part of a larger study on the classroom identities of first year pupils in an urban comprehensive school as capable or incapable school learners (Monk 1981). In this part of the work an attempt was made to quickly and cheaply test the classroom climate for any one pupil or group of pupils by simply asking the children what they thought about their peers.

3.5.2 The Nature of the Data

The questionnaire that the children received consisted of a single sheet of paper down the left hand side of which were listed the names of every child in that particular class. The names were arranged according to groupings that had been elicited through the prior administration of a sociometric questionnaire. So on the list groups of friends appeared clustered together. Assured of confidentiality the children were asked to write alongside each and every name what they thought of that particular classmate. Some children just wrote single words. Others listed personal attributes or general responses, whilst others wrote complete sentences about their peers. When the questionnaires were collected back there were for each class 28 or so sheets of paper each with comments on the 28 or so members of the class. These comments were transferred to a single large sheet of paper, one for each class, where they filled the cells of a matrix whose two axes were the writers (senders) of the comments and the pupils to whom the comments were directed (receivers).

By reading down the columns of the matrix, all the comments made about any one individual could be read off. By reading across any row of the matrix, all the comments one pupil had made about his classmates could be read.

3.5.3 Development of the Categories of the Network

Figure 3.5.1 (overleaf) shows the categories developed to describe the responses. Their meaning is now discussed.

On reading the comments that the children had written it was all too clear that quite a considerable number were vague and general, only indicating predispositions. So comments like "Okay", "nice", "good friend", "hate", were seen to constitute a category of comments to do with LIKING, and this was further subdivided into MILD and STRONG. A comment like "Don't have much to do with him" was not taken to give an indication of any liking as such but rather DISTANCED sender from receiver. LIKING and DISTANCING were subsumed under FEELINGS at the less delicate level.

The difference between "nice" and "hate" is not just one of mild versus strong. They are different in terms of being POSITIVELY accepting or NEGATIVELY rejecting. This dichotomy was introduced into the network as a co-selection through the less delicate category POLARITY. It was recognised that some comments might carry uncertainty, or even ambivalence towards the recipient of the comment. Some allowance could have been made for this by developing more delicate categories of POLARITY that would have reflected these differences. However in the event it was decided that a clear distinction would make the analysis simpler even at the cost of a certain amount of oversimplification. The data itself was not particularly sophisticated nor especially controlled in its range. It was felt that more could be gained than lost with this simple dichotomous division.

Comments like "handsome" or "looks like a muppet" were self evidently to do with APPEARANCE. These were counted with comments on SKILLS at the less delicate level in the category PHYSICAL. SKILLS was used to code comments on swimming, athletics and sports in general.

Not too surprisingly the children made comments about the day to day CLASSROOM PROCESSES in which they and their peers were caught up. These comments were divided into two major categories; those to do with COGNITIVE processes and those to do with BEHAVIOURAL aspects. The COGNITIVE aspects were again divided into two; those to do with ABILITY such as "brainy" or "dim" etc. and those to do with EFFORT such as "works hard", "just doesn't try". The BEHAVIOURAL aspects were made more delicate with two terminal categories: those to do with the OTHER ONLY such as "chews", "chatters", and those to do with the WHOLE CLASS such as "plays about" or "very noisy".

Lastly a category was introduced at the least delicate level to take account of the comments that appeared to be reporting interactions rather than feelings. The INTERACTION category was divided through two further levels of delicacy. At the first there is ASSOCIATION and DOMINATION and at the second level EMPATHY, FUN, VERBAL, PHYSICAL, and LEADERSHIP. The EMPATHY terminal was used to code comments such as "understanding", "helps me" or NEGATIVELY "tells tales", "bitchy". The FUN terminal in the POSITIVE sense should be self explanatory. In the NEGATIVE sense, "fool", "silly" would be coded under FUN. EMPATHY and FUN are ASSOCIATIVE types of comment. PHYSICAL, VERBAL, LEADERSHIP are more to do with DOMINATION. VERBAL was used to code "bighead", "show-off" as well as "loudmouth", and in the POSITIVE sense, "nice to talk to". PHYSICAL was used to code comments such as "bully", or "thinks he's tough".

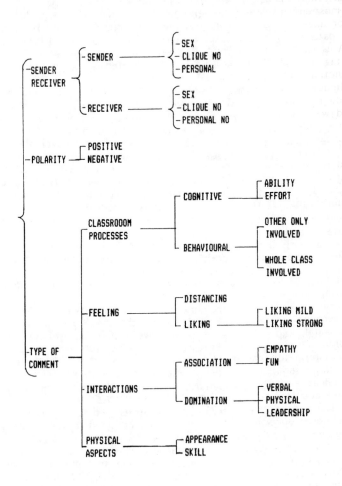

Figure 3.5.1   Final network for children's comments

3.5.4 Managing the Data for Analysis

In order to be able to use BARBARA, the computer programme developed by F. Grize to handle network data, some further network description was required so as to organise the sorting of the data. The most obvious categories to suggest themselves are those of the two major axes of the data matrices themselves SENDER and RECEIVER. The data requires description in both of these categories and so a BRA is used to link them. It was convenient to apply three labels to tag the SENDER and RECEIVER. These were determined by predictions of what sortings might usefully be explored and were applicable to both the sender and the receiver. So the SEX of the child, the NUMBER allocated to the CLIQUE of friends that the child was associated with, and finally a PERSONAL NUMBER as a member of the class, were all used. There is a fair amount of redundancy in this in that a PERSONAL NUMBER would suffice but this redundancy does help considerably when sorting the data. In building up new groupings it is often quicker to redefine the groups from cliques, sex and personal numbers than to list all group members. The trade off was in requiring extra code against the possibility of future more complex questioning. It was thought to be one worth making.

3.5.5 Sorting the Data Ready for Further Analysis

The intention in developing the network was that finally some form of counting should be carried out. For the counting to be a worthwhile exercise the number of comments that would, on average, be assigned to any terminal category therefore needed to be such that statistical work could be carried out with some confidence. Having about 28 children in each class, something like 900 comments could be expected. With 14 terminal categories in the descriptive part of the network, 28 when the polarity is considered, the delicacy to which the network is pursued appears to be about right. In fact the terminals do not all receive equal counts, as is shown in Table 3.5.1.

This profile across the terminals gives us some indication of how the children spontaneously react and think about each other. Their liking or disliking of their fellows is the most important aspect of the classroom climate which these children in class A produce, and then react to. Perhaps not too surprisingly for eleven year olds the PHYSICAL terms of APPEARANCE and SKILL receive few counts. The profile is likely to be rather different for 15 to 16 year olds. And indeed it is to be expected that some aspects of the network would poorly serve analysis of a similar nature with a different group of pupils.

Suppose we decide to divide the data in the matrix by sex. We might want to find out if the boys and girls are separately described in similar ways by the class as a whole. Or we might want to ask if the boys talk about their peers in ways that are different from the ways in which the girls talk about the other children in the class.

CATEGORY	POS.	NEG.	TOTAL
ABILITY	31	12	43
EFFORT	14	4	18
ONLY OTHER INVOLVED	11	37	48
WHOLE CLASS INVOLVED	63	30	93
DISTANCING	7	9	16
LIKING MILD	263	23	286
LIKING STRONG	50	39	89
EMPATHY	57	74	131
FUN	71	67	138
VERBAL	11	44	55
PHYSICAL	0	38	38
LEADERSHIP	3	10	13
APPEARANCE	1	11	12
SKILL	13	1	14
TOTAL	595	399	994

Table 3.5.1   Counts at the terminals for Class A

Another question could be to ask if the girls talk about themselves in similar terms to the ways in which the boys talk about themselves. Such questions can be answered by simply re-grouping the SENDERS and RECEIVERS of the comments. The managerial aspect of the network when used in conjunction with BARBARA makes this sort of questioning both rapid and straightforward once the required groupings of SENDERS and RECEIVERS have been defined.

Using the co-selections of POLARITY and SENDER/RECEIVER allows the counts at each terminal in the part of the network giving types of comment to be broken down to give values that can fill the cells of a contingency table. Sorting the data by sex will give 2X2 contingency tables with the dimensions of girls-boys/positive-negative comments. Association and statistical significance can be tested within each of these tables.

Taking a straightforward cross product measure (log alpha) it was possible to test each contingency table for association between positive comments being directed at the girls and negative comments being directed at the boys.

Because counts are combined when moving up the branches of the network to the left at less delicate levels it is possible to construct similar contingency tables for each and every term of the network. Where strong association and statistical significance is found at one level of delicacy it may vanish, due to the combining process, at less delicate levels.

3.5.6 Life in Class A

In this particular class the boys were seen as being more disruptive than the girls. They were also seen as being generally sillier in their behaviour and less fun than the girls, as well as more domineering in their interactions. At the 0.05 level of significance they were not seen as being any more or less capable as classroom learners, nor were they seen as being any different with respect to physical attributes or general likeability. These things one could have perhaps guessed. What one was less likely to be able to guess was that the overall classroom climate in class A was marginally more accepting of the girls than of the boys. Figure 3.5.2 shows those categories for which there is a significant association (terms for which the association is significant at the 0.05 level are highlighted).

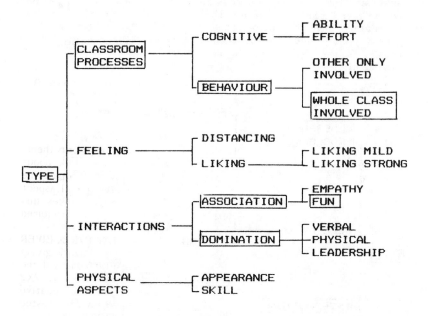

Figure 3.5.2   Significant categories for girls/
boys - positive/negative comments

The division into boys and girls was built into the managerial part of the network as a feature because it was anticipated that such questioning would be used. It was also anticipated that some questioning according to perceived classroom abilities as capable school learners would be used to order and sort the data matrix. This was not built into the managerial part of the network and the groupings had to be separately defined according to a ranking scheme that had previously been constructed after a series of interviews with a selection of the children. With this ranking scheme the data was sorted to give values to fill the cells of 2x2 contingency tables with the dimensions of peer perceived capable-incapable classroom learners versus positive-negative comments.

Again the level of significance was set at 0.05 and a measure of association between the top half and positive comments and the bottom half and negative comments was taken. As might be expected these results confirm some commonsense views of the classroom. The children in this particular class recognised their more capable peers as well as those that they thought were less capable of classroom learning. The bottom children were generally reckoned to be more behaviourally disruptive both in terms of the whole class and their personal actions. The top people were seen as being fun whilst the bottom people were seen as silly. The top people were seen as less dominating than the bottom ones, and finally the top people were generally more liked by the class as a whole than were the bottom people. Figure 3.5.3 shows the categories for which the association was significant.

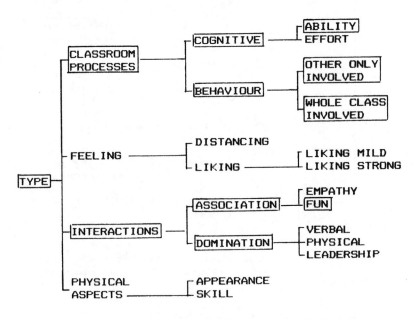

Figure 3.5.3   Significant categories for peer reported classroom achievement and polarity of comment

From this analysis of the data it could be argued that because the more capable classroom learners lived in a more accepting environment, created as part of the classroom climate by the children themselves, they would probably flourish. The children reported by their peers to be less capable classroom learners were daily confirmed in that role by their interactions with their peers.

3.5.7 Concluding Remark

Through the use of a network analysis it has been possible to more closely approach the children's own world within the classroom. The network analysis has allowed free responses, and quite a sizable number at that, to be efficiently handled so that it has even been possible to carry out some statistical tests for association. I think that this is a gain that is not to be lightly dismissed.

3.6 PROBLEM SOLVING BY CHEMISTRY STUDENTS

by Paul Black and Harry Elliott

3.6.1 Aim and Design of the Research

In this example, a network has been developed to handle data obtained from students' attempts to solve problems. The aim of the research is to describe the procedures that students, specialising at sixth form or freshman level in physical sciences, use in tackling routine problems that test their power to apply standard methods and basic principles.

Six different problems were used, distributed amongst sixteen students so that each student attempted four. The problems were composed in pairs to explore the effects of several types of difference between problems: content area, structuring of the task and qualitative or quantitative form. The details are not relevant here, except that the research plan required that the same or very similar networks be used so that it would be possible to make comparisons between the work on different problems.

3.6.2 Obtaining the Data

A problem was presented on paper to an individual student, who was asked to work on his own, without interruption, until he had finished or could go no further. The student was asked to write down his calculations and solutions in the way that he usually would, and to take as much time as he needed. Immediately on finishing, he was interviewed by the researcher. The interview was followed by a tutorial during which the researcher attempted to correct any misconceptions that the student had and discussions evolved around the various approaches to solving the problem.

The interview had three phases. The first phase was meant to elicit what the student did by way of reading, re-reading, analysing and appraising the problem when it was read, how clearly he perceived its demands, whether he felt the need of a text book or notes for reference, and what he was thinking about just before getting started.

In the second phase, the interviewer tried to reconstruct the solution referring to the student's written record, and asking of each step in the solution how, when and why it was done. This phase produced on average about 40 questions.

The third and final phase explored the student's confidence about reaching or having reached the solution, and asked about his experience of similar problems, his opinions about other forms in which the same or similar problems might be set, and any explicit instruction in general methods for tackling problems he might have had.

The interviews were not designed to test any explicit theory of problem solving, except for the belief that the initial appraisal on reading the problem, and the student's appraisal of his efforts at the end, would be significant. Changes of approach en route, and intermediate evaluations were questioned thoroughly.

3.6.3 Constructing a Network

This account concerns only the second phase of the interview which gave a record of the sequence of operations undertaken to transform the data in order to produce the required solution, together with the student's account of these activities in terms of their perceived nature and function within his solution strategy. Section 3.6.3.1 concerns the analysis of the solution routes whilst Section 3.6.3.2 is an account of the network and coding used to describe the complete protocol of this second phase, of which the solution route forms one component.

3.6.3.1 Solution Routes

This part of the work can be illustrated by considering one of the problems. It is a fairly standard calculation which might appear in an A-level Chemistry test:

> A sample of gas containing only nitrogen and oxygen has a mass of 66.0 grams and occupies a volume of 36.7 cubic decimetres (litres) at a temperature of 298 K and 101.3 kPa (1.0 atm.). Deduce the empirical (simplest) formula of this gas containing nitrogen and oxygen.

The solution required is the formula N_2O showing that there are two atoms of nitrogen to every one of oxygen in the gas. One approach which can be used is to transform the data given to obtain the masses of oxygen and of nitrogen in the original gas, and then by using molar masses of the two elements (which could be obtained from the periodic table supplied) to deduce the relative numbers of atoms.

A pilot scrutiny of solutions by 25 students showed that there were a large number of routes to the solution of the problem. This is possible because there is a very large number of ways of transforming the given data. Standard rules can be used to transform the volume of nitrogen produced at 298K and 1.0 atm. to, for example

> the volume at 273K and 1.0 atm.
> the volume yield from unit mass (say 1 g) of gas
> the number of moles of nitrogen gas

(A mole is a quantity containing a standard number of molecules, and the volume of a mole at 273K and 1 atm. is a well-known piece of data.)

Combinations of these yield further possibilities. These facts led to the idea of representing all possible transformations as a map of the 'problem space', so that an individual solution (whether correct or not) could be represented as the selection of a particular path through that space.

A first map depicting correct solutions was drawn up and a second one was needed for incorrect solutions. The basis for a map consisted of boxes (nodes) connected by lines (links), where the nodes represented physical quantities given or derived whilst the lines represented transformations whereby data from one or more boxes are combined or transformed to give a new quantity. A typical node might be the mass of a sample of material and this might be divided (link) by a second node, the volume of the same sample, to yield a new node, the density of the material. The task of mapping the problem space becomes a problem of representing all possible nodes and links.

These maps were extremely complex and tended to hinder analysis. It was then noticed that each node could be described completely by three aspects:

a statement of a MEASURE (e.g. mass; volume)
a description of the SUBSTANCE (e.g. the sample; molecular oxygen)
the REFERENCE conditions (e.g. at 298K or at 273K)

Although a three-dimensional representation could now be made of these nodes the network in Figure 3.6.1 is an equivalent representation of these three aspects. Each node is represented by a legitimate string of terminals from the network.

A second network, not discussed here, though fairly straightfoward, was drawn up to describe the links referred to in the above mentioned maps. With the use of these two networks it was then

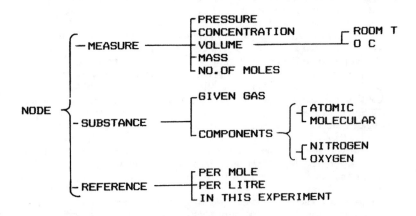

Figure 3.6.1   Network representation of a node

possible to represent a solution as a sequence of:

    NODE or NODES:
    OPERATED ON BY A LINK:
    TO YIELD A NEW NODE

To represent the whole of this operation in a network required consideration of ways to describe the solver's actions. Such consideration alters the above to:

    SELECTED   A NODE :
    OPERATED   A LINK :
    OBTAINED   A NODE or NODES

in which the emphasised verbs must be selected from a set of labels which represent the solver's actions on the data of the problem. These were later termed DIRECT actions.

Thus the network developed into the outline in Figure 3.6.2. The set of actions distinguished between: choosing from given data (SELECTED); bringing in of data or links not given (IMPORTED); using results obtained within the work so far (CALLED); employing some specified link operation (OPERATED); and producing a new node (OBTAINED). A typical sequence would be:

    SELECTED X,
    SELECTED Y,
    IMPORTED Z,
    OPERATED Z,
    OBTAINED W

where X, Y and W would be nodes and Z a link.

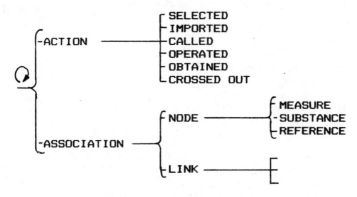

Figure 3.6.2   Part of network related to problem solver's actions

The network in Figure 3.6.2 allows meaningless combinations e.g. operated mass of gas per experiment. This will have to be remembered if the frequency with which possible combinations occur is compared with (say) the random (chance) frequency. The possibility could be avoided by changing to the form in Figure 3.6.3. This was not done because it was judged that the action labels represented properties common to use of nodes and links which would be lost if separate lists were set up as required by Figure 3.6.3.

3.6.3.2 The Full Network

The complete protocols contained far more than the account of the solution routes, so the network discussed in Section 3.6.3.1 had to be embedded in a larger network capable of describing all the features.

The following account attempts to describe the network as briefly as possible; it does not give a complete history of its evolution although specific points are discussed.

In order to convey some idea of the nature of the data and to illustrate the subsequent discussion, the following outline of one protocol (about a different chemistry problem) is first presented as an informal prose summary.

Protocol Outline

(a) The student stated that he first scanned the problem statement to see what it was about.

(b) He then read it twice more stopping and going back and forth.

(c) He then read it carefully again to pick out the data needed to solve the problem.

(d) Next he worked through one piece of calculation.

(e) Then he worked through another calculation.

(f) Then he stopped to look for faults because he thought he had gone wrong.

(g) He crossed out the suspect result.

(h) He next made a different calculation using one of his previous results.

(i) Thinking about the result of this move, he decided that he was nearly home.

(j) A further calculation starting from the result of (h) yielded the required result.

(k) He then felt pleased with his achievement.

The first decision of the analysis was to organise the protocol into a time sequence divided into units (called 'moves'). In the example above, the moves are described by the sentences (a) to (k). Each 'move' was to be represented by a separate line in the coding.

The next decision was to categorise these units into three main types, as represented by the network in Figure 3.6.4: EXECUTION DIRECT, EXECUTION INDIRECT, CONTROL.

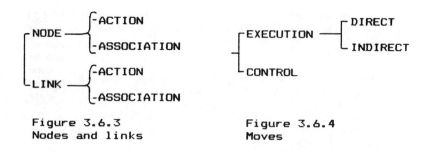

Figure 3.6.3
Nodes and links

Figure 3.6.4
Moves

Insofar as a model of problem-solving forms the basis of analysis its main feature is that the solver is regarded as operating on the two levels of EXECUTION and CONTROL. These two levels are now discussed in greater detail.

EXECUTION DIRECT: These are moves of the type described in Section 3.6.3.1, lines (d)(e)(g)(h) and (j) being in this category. Using a network very like that in Figure 3.6.2, the full coding for line (d) of this example came out as

> SELECTED MOL IONIC Sr PER DM ,
> SELECTED RTP CPD PER PROBLEM,
> IMPORTED MOL FR CONC/VOL
> OPERATED MOL FR CONC/VOL
> OBTAINED MOL IONIC Sr PER PROBLEM.

This will be simplified for presentation in the rest of this section as:

> SELECTED (node),
> SELECTED (node),
> IMPORTED (link),
> OPERATED (link),
> OBTAINED (new node).

A typical line would be a sequence of EXECUTION DIRECT labels ending with an OBTAINED label.

EXECUTION INDIRECT: Lines (a)(b) and (c) above are examples in this category. Examples of actions we have termed 'indirect' are reading and internally constructing a route or partial solution to the problem. Such actions are described as doing something (ACTION e.g. Read-Scanned) with or to something (ASSOCIATION e.g. part of the question) in a certain way (DESCRIPTOR e.g. twice).

CONTROL: Examples of CONTROL statements are lines (f)(i)(k). These CONTROL moves are concerned with COMP-REHENSION of the problem; with PLANNING the next moves in the solutions; or with evaluating (TRACING) or searching for errors in (DEBUGGING) work already completed. These different labels classify each CONTROL move according to its purpose.

Apart only from the specification of the nodes and links involved in EXECUTION DIRECT, the network for all of the problems is the same, so that it is not possible to tell, from the second (simplified) version of the SELECTED--OBTAINED episode set out above, to which problem it refers. This was done so that the protocols for the different types of problem could be compared through analyses of their codes. It would of course have been possible to develop a distinct network for each problem. The discussion of the ways in which solutions varied with problem type would then have included comparisons of the networks which had to be developed to serve for each type. However, it was clear that such discussion would also have had to compare coding frequencies and patterns and that such comparisons would be indirect if these derived from different networks. Thus a common network which relegated comparisons to analysis of codes would simplify the task provided that such a network did not force the representations to make the protocols appear more similar than they were. The critical judgment here was that the common network that evolved did not have this disadvantage.

The full network is illustrated in Figure 3.6.5.

Since it is anticipated that a further analysis of the codings will be important in this work, the coding that will follow from Figure 3.6.5 is illustrated. For the protocol described informally above, keeping to the corresponding lines (a) to (k), the code reads:

(a)   SCANNED COMPLETE ONCE SMOOTH
(b)   SYSTEMATISED COMPLETE TWICE BACKTRACKING
(c)   SYSTEMATISED COMPLETE ONCE SMOOTH
(d) SELECTED, SELECTED, IMPORTED, OPERATED, OBTAINED
(e) CALLED, SELECTED, RE-IMPORTED, RE-OPERATED,
        OBTAINED
(f)   EXPLICIT COMPREHENSION:
            EVALUATED ACTUAL PART NOT SURE
(g) CROSSED OUT
(h) RESELECTED, CALLED, IMPORTED, OPERATED, OBTAINED
(i)   EXPLICIT PLANNING: REALISED FINAL CLOSE
(j) SELECTED, CALLED, IMPORTED, OPERATED, OBTAINED
(k)   EXPLICIT TRACING: FELT SURE PLEASED

For ease of reading, the three main types of move are distinguished by three types of identation; full width for EXECUTION DIRECT, a single indent for EXECUTION INDIRECT and a double indent for CONTROL. DESCRIPTOR labels were only needed very occasionally for DIRECT ACTIONS so the NIL label was not used since it would have appeared so often (e.g. five times in line d).

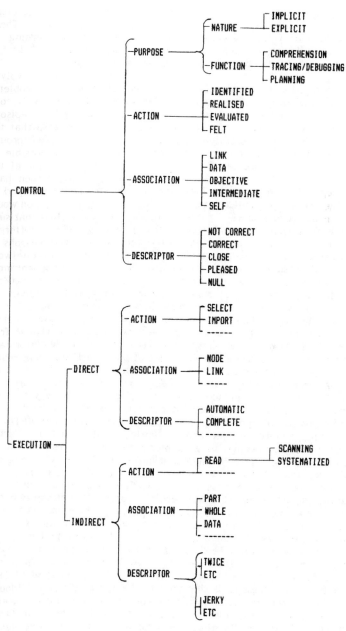

Figure 3.6.5   Complete problem solving network

3.6.4 Commentary

At the time of writing, a collection of codes is being made using the (now hopefully stable) network. It is clear that many different analyses of the codes may be made. Some examples are

> the relative frequency of control to execution lines.
> the statistics of the sequencing of control, direct, indirect
>> sequences in the codes (are there natural rhythms?).
> the link between the form of the problem and the length of
>> the direct execution chains.
> consistency in pattern of the same solver across four
>> different problems.

and so on. It is too early to estimate whether any such analyses will yield features of particular interest.

The network is a very detailed one and the codes that it yields will be extensive and very close in form to ordered prose summaries of the protocols. This has arisen partly because the protocols were complicated and yet judged to be rich in their details, so that it seemed important to capture this detail. However, there is a deeper reason which may throw more light on the function of the network in the research. There are various accounts and models of problem-solving in existence. It would have been possible to use these to draw up a broad typology of solution strategies and then use this as a category system giving a less detailed network. For example, one such strategy is "backward reasoning". However, only a small number of the protocols are completely clear examples of backward reasoning whilst others contain smaller patches of such a strategy mixed with other types of approach. Generally it was felt that the various models that do exist could not do justice to the data, partly because they were not based on detailed empirical studies on this type of problem - indeed many do not appear to relate to any extensive empirical basis at all. Had a more detailed and appropriate model existed, it could have been used as the basis for a simpler network, but one main motive for the research- to provide the empirical basis which was lacking for the development of just such a model- would have disappeared.

One consequence of this scenario is that some of the burden of extracting significance from the results is shifted from the network to the coding and analysis of codes. To put the matter in an extreme form, it is possible that analysis of the codes could lead to formulation of new typologies, which could be used to compose a simpler, more powerful, more theory-bound network, which could itself yield simpler codes. This last state would then have moved the emphasis back into the network. It follows that the theory underlying this network at present is limited to the CONTROL/EXECUTION model which forms the basis of the network. But it is not being used as a Baconian induction machine, and it could have a powerful influence on the results that could arise from the research.

3.7   USING NETWORKS TO REPRESENT PUPILS' MEANINGS
FOR CONCEPTS OF FORCE AND ENERGY

by D. Michael Watts

3.7.1   Introduction

In this paper I deal with the use of the network notation to portray some individual meanings that schoolchildren have for some words denoting concepts in school science. Typically, youngsters have distinct idiosyncratic interpretations for terms like gravity, heat, light, force and energy. These last two are expressions that permeate current school curricula and are prerequisite for an understanding of much of physics.

To anyone used to talking to children in schools the variety and ingenuity of their world-views will come as no surprise. They bring to lessons their own explanatory models for many of the common phenomena that science would hope to explain. Clearly, the views expressed by pupils will frequently be at odds with orthodox (textbook) science. Here, I have adopted the term 'alternative frameworks' to denote the personal, imaginative interpretations that youngsters construct, a term taken from the work of Driver and Easley (1978).

The focus of my discussion will be pupils' alternative frameworks for force and energy. To explore these meanings and generate the data, I have used a research technique called the Interview-about-Instances method (Osborne and Gilbert, 1979; Gilbert, Watts and Osborne, 1981). In outline, the technique consists of tape recorded dyadic discussions with a pupil using a set of pictures (line drawings) on cards as a focus. The deck of cards concerns the application of one word. The drawings consist of sketches of familiar situations which may, or may not, represent an example of the application of the word. Whatever the student's response, a reason is sought. A concept, then, is seen as having a 'range of convenience', a range of instances where it is appropriate for the user to apply the concept.

As an illustration I have chosen the word force. A physicist, for example, might find it appropriate to use the word force in a discussion about gravitational effects, but not about temperature effects. The latter lie outside the concept's range. Even within it, some situations may be examples of the concept, others non-examples. Friction is an example of force; pressure is not. So far, this discussion can be represented by Figure 3.7.1.

Some of the results of the study - pupils' alternative frameworks of force and gravity - have been reported elsewhere (Watts and Zylbersztajn, 1980; Watts, 1982; Watts, 1982b). Examples of the cards are given in Figure 3.7.2.

With the Instances-about-Interview technique each of the interviews is in itself a significant study of individual meaning. I have used networks principally as a heuristic device to clarify and chart a person's meaning for particular concepts. The network that

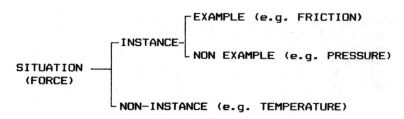

Figure 3.7.1   Application of "range of convenience"

a.   A golfer hitting a golf ball.
     Are there any forces here?

b. The golf ball about to land in the hole.
   Are there any forces here?

Figure 3.7.2   Cards related to concept of force

results from this analysis I have called 'idiographic'. From a broader consideration of the data it is possible to detect common meanings across a number of interviews. These alternative frameworks can also be represented by networks, as I have attempted in Section 3.7.4. Finally a managerial type of network maps out the organisation of the research approach (Figure 3.7.8).

3.7.2 Energy and Force: Types of Relation Between Them

Turning now to the pupils' ideas about energy and force, there are three possible ways in which these are talked about:

1. Entirely separate and unrelated (in that the ranges-of-convenience do not overlap). For example:

> J Now let me think ... force is moving object .. or moving things ... and energy ... well, you have to have energy and store it ... and then use it up. You can get energy from oil ... petrol ... the sun ... anything that's got it. (03.16).

In this example 'force' is associated with movement whilst 'energy' is something one possesses, in fuels etc.

2. Separate but interconnected (there is some overlap). For example, when posed with the 'golfer' card ("are there any forces here?"), one fifteen year old said of the golfball:

> S Well ... only the force of gravity making it move ... and the forces of energy that make it travel. (01.15)

3. Synonymous and interchangeable. For example,

> S Yes ... force is the energy from one thing into another ... if you push something you are pushing energy from you into the thing and it'll start going ... moving. (04.17)

These three possibilities can be represented as in Figure 3.7.3 Details of pupils quoted in this paper are given in Table 3.7.1.

	NAME	AGE	PHYSICS GROUP	NUMBER
1	SARAH	15	O-LEVEL	(01.15)
2	PAT	15	O-LEVEL	(02.15)
3	JULIE	16	CSE	(03.16)
4	STEVE	17	A-LEVEL	(04.17)

Table 3.7.1   Pupils in Study

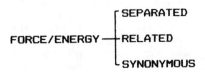

FORCE/ENERGY
- SEPARATED
- RELATED
- SYNONYMOUS

Figure 3.7.3   Major distinctions for
force and energy

3.7.3 Example of an Idiographic Network for Force and Energy

The following extract looks at the case where the pupil's ideas of force and energy are separate. The pupil, Pat (P), discusses these in relation to instances concerning the golfer and the golfball.

I Well ... what's the difference then between umh ... force and energy?

P Well energy has got to run out sometime ... because it's powered by something ... some fuel or, it's hit by something ... so it's got to run out.

I I see, so ...

P You've only got a certain amount of energy and once you've used that up you can't get it back again ... unless you hit it again or fuel it up again.

I Do you mean the golfball?

P Yes. As soon as he hits it its got the most energy because it can ... well when it's in mid-air ... it's on the verge of losing energy and so it starts to fall down, but when it's just struck at the beginning it's full of energy and so it moves as high as it can.

I And what about force?

P Well force is the way you ... well if you put force on something you could push it ... pull it ... tug at it .. you could move it in a certain way...The way you want to move it and so ... I mean you could push it and pull it any way you want to ... but energy has got to be refuelled ... it'll run out of fuel eventually so its something that only lasts a certain time ...whereas force can last as long as it wants to really ...as long as it's pushing or pulling. (O2.15)

One of the major difficulties in writing an idiographic network comes in trying to paraphrase sections of transcript in order to capture essential features and yet retain some elements of the children's own language. In essence Pat pictures force as a maintained activity and energy as a consumable property: both are popular ways of describing the two concepts. A summary of her arguments about the golfball's energy can be framed into the following statements:

the golfball receives a quantity of energy from the golf club.
it needs this energy for its upward movement in flight.
from its maximum height downwards it begins to lose its energy.
something with energy has to be replenished (with fuel, rehit or powered).

Her arguments can be represented by a network as in Figure 3.7.4.

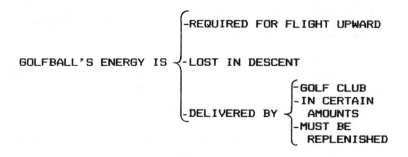

GOLFBALL'S ENERGY IS
- REQUIRED FOR FLIGHT UPWARD
- LOST IN DESCENT
- DELIVERED BY
    - GOLF CLUB
    - IN CERTAIN AMOUNTS
    - MUST BE REPLENISHED

Figure 3.7.4   Idiographic network for energy

Pat's ideas about force can be summarised as:

an intentional activity.
a push, a pull or a tug.
produces movement.
lasts as long as is required.

This list is represented in Figure 3.7.5.
The network in Figure 3.7.5 shows that Pat's ideas about force are more general than her ideas about energy. She does not tie the notion of force to the golfball's force but rather tends to see it in a more de-contextualised sense. Putting these two meanings together gives an idiographic network which could take a form somewhat like that shown in Figure 3.7.6.

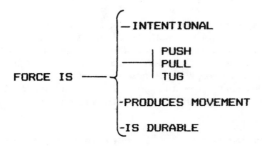

Figure 3.7.5   Idiographic network for force

In the interview Pat eventually decided that neither of the two instances were examples of her concept of force, but that they were both about energy.

The construction of this kind of network is particularly useful in order to question and structure individual accounts. They represent what youngsters think but say it in only a limited way: they are my attempts to map out their ideas.

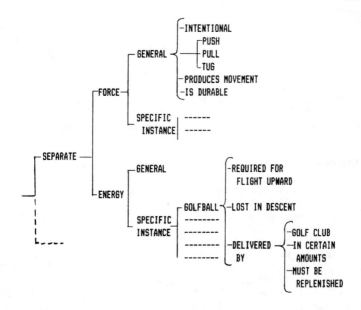

Figure 3.7.6   Idiographic network combining ideas of force and energy

3.7.4 Network for an Alternative Framework for Energy

Alternative frameworks for energy, each of which attempts to capture meanings shared by a number of children, have been identified in the transcripts. One of these, which I have called 'depositary', 'D' frameworks, is described in the next paragraph.

In this framework energy is seen as an entity that can be transmitted from object to object. Some objects are naturally endowed with quantities of energy; other objects can suffer deficits and need energy in order to function. This kind of framework gives rise to many teleological arguments: the objects that need energy do so because it is in their nature to do so. Objects that neither have nor require energy, again, can operate quite 'naturally'. Force is sometimes the mechanism by which energy is transmitted: energy is forced out of one object into another that needs it, or forces an object to move. A further consequence of this framework is that when a surplus (positive) amount of energy is realised by a deficient (negative) object, then the ensuing action 'cancels out' the energy and it is 'used up'. An attempt to map out these ideas gives the network in Figure 3.7.7.

The symbol 'D' now becomes shorthand for all the complex set of meanings associated with this 'depositary' framework. Several alternative frameworks representing the most popular models used by pupils have also been identified although there is not the space to describe them here. These are signified by P Q R and so on, in the managerial network in Figure 3.7.8.

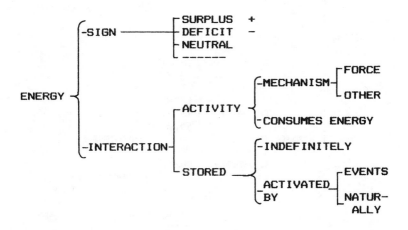

Figure 3.7.7   Network for Depositary Framework 'D'

In order to get an overall view of what happens in the research, the network in Figure 3.7.8 puts together a number of ideas. Firstly, there is the description of the range of convenience of a situation (see network in Figure 3.7.1). Secondly, the area under discussion is indicated and lastly the potential set of choices involved in children's responses is illustrated.

3.7.5 Summary

In this study I have mainly used networks to sort out individuals' meanings for particular ideas. However I have also attempted to use them as a tentative representation of an alternative framework for energy. As it is the network is a gross, 'indelicate' caricature of the sorts of things children say. However, it has the advantage of attempting to capture in an economical and graphical manner what is typical to several answers. More to the point, by presenting a pithy collective viewpoint in this way, it can allow teachers quick and useful insights into children's thinking. The identification, analysis and representation of alternative frameworks has major implications for the successful engagement of children in the learning of physics.

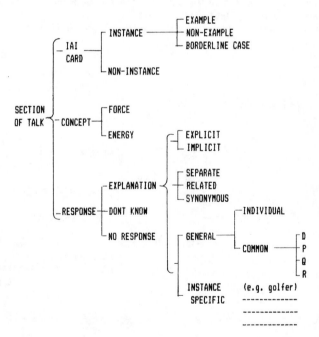

Figure 3.7.8   Attempt at managerial network

3.8 USE OF A NETWORK FOR ITEM-BANKING

by Jon Ogborn

3.8.1 Introduction

The storage of large numbers of examination or test questions, in such a way that questions (henceforth 'items') with given characteristics can be retrieved, is an important practical problem in education. For some years the writer was responsible for the multiple choice questions used in the Nuffield Advanced Level Physics examination and the use of a network for banking these items described here was a pilot attempt to improve the banking system. In brief, each item is described by a code, with a network storing the possible coding terms for items. The network and codes employ the computer system BARBARA described in the Appendix. Although this application of networks has not yet been implemented it seems worth describing in view of the potential benefits such a method appears to offer.

3.8.2 Conventional Item-Banking

Most item banks use a rather simple system for recording information about items. In addition to statistical data, such as the difficulty and discrimination of the item, and its dates of use, source, correct answer, etc., it is clearly necessary to record some indication of its content and preferably of the type of ability it seems to call for. Commonly, the content is indicated simply as the syllabus section to which the item belongs: thus items about simple direct current circuits and items about alternating current circuits could be labelled as belonging to the 'electricity' section of the syllabus, probably by reference to a section number. Similarly, the categories for the ability called for by the item are generally fairly simple, often based on some adaptation of Bloom's taxonomy of educational objectives. Thus items might be labelled as requiring 'knowledge', 'comprehension', 'application', and so forth.

The majority of item banking systems use simple, single-level category schemes. Thus the computer input for content is just one out of a number of codes each covering some range of subject matter; similarly for types of ability called for. In consequence, it is only the users of the bank, and not the computer system, who know the connections between different kinds of content or ability code. Only the users know, for example, that direct current circuits relate both to questions about electric potential in a field, and to electromagnetic induction, if it happens that these last belong to differently coded syllabus sections. One purpose of the present application of networks is to remedy this kind of defect, enabling one to recover items described by a variety of labels whose interrelationships are 'known' to the computer system.

A second goal is to make the descriptions of items more 'natural', that is, more nearly in accord with the intuitions of teachers or pupils. This means describing items more at their face value, for example as about magnets, or as about dynamos, and not by more abstract labels - particularly not by arbitrary syllabus sections.

It may be, of course, that a syllabus is divided in so natural a way as to make such work unnecessary. This was certainly not the case for the Nuffield A-level course, in which topics were repeated through the course in varied guises and in which the divisions of the course into units of work did not reflect the structure of the ideas they contained. This feature, felt to be educationally desirable in the structure of the course, meant that items 'belonging' to different units could nevertheless have much in common, and that sometimes it was even impossible to assign items to a unit. It was also desirable to encourage items to be produced which synthesised ideas from different parts of the course, and the labelling of items by only one part would at the least not offer such encouragement. This last argument seems likely to apply to cases other than Nuffield Physics.

Further, there is evidence that teachers and examiners find it hard to apply reliably most of the various schemes for categorising abilities required by questions. The difficulty is that high level descriptors such as 'Application' do not relate closely enough to what they perceive the question as requiring pupils to do, or to what they feel the nature of its difficulties to be. Whilst labels such as 'requiring a simple calculation' might meet this last criterion, one then has the problem that several such are needed for each question and that the immediacy of the label sacrifices any level of generality of kind of educational demand.

It was to meet these and related problems that the system described here was developed. After some ten years of operation, the Nuffield A-level Physics examiners had some 400 items previously used, and a similar number in various stages of preparation, so that a practical problem of banking certainly existed (and was solved in the short term in the conventional way), whilst in addition a substantial and coherent body of material on which to test the ideas was readily available.

3.8.3 Descriptions of Some Questions

Consider the two pairs of items shown in Figure 3.8.1. The first pair are similar in both being about fields, but differ in that one concerns a gravitational field and the other an electric field. To the eye of the physicist they are really very similar, in that both deal with (approximately) uniform fields, and share the same methods of calculation, though the second happens to ask about forces and the first about potential - a situation that could have been reversed. The second pair, concerning cars rolling down a hill, could appear to have little in common with the first pair, but in fact are related more closely than the fact that the word 'potential' appears in both would indicate. Like the first two, the problems can best be understood by considering the energy changes produced by the action of

7,8

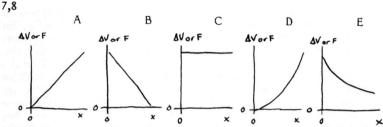

7   Which one of the above graphs best indicates the relationship between ΔV, the change in gravitational potential energy of a spacecraft, and its height x above the surface of the Earth, during the first 100 m after launching?

8   Which one of the above graphs best indicates the relationship between the force F on an electron in the electric field between two oppositely charged large parallel plates, and the perpendicular distance x from the electron to one of the plates?

9,10

Two identical lengths of smooth toy racing-car track are arranged as shown. They start and stop at the same heights, but curve differently. A friction-free car is rolled down each in turn, starting from rest at the top. Student X argues correctly that the car will leave the bottom of both tracks at the same speed. Student Y argues correctly that the car will take longer to run down (a) than (b).
    Which one of the remarks A to E would help

9   to show that Student X is correct?
10 to show that Student Y is correct?

    A   The car travels the same distance along both tracks, so it must gain the same kinetic energy.
    B   The change in potential energy of the car is the same on both occasions.
    C   The acceleration of the car is the same on both occasions.
    D   The faster the car goes near the start, the less time it will take to cover lower parts of the track.
    E   The final momentum of the car will be larger if the time of travel is longer.

Figure 3.8.1   Two pairs of items
(by permission: Oxford and Cambridge Schools Examination Board)

forces. The last question contains something the other three do not, namely a need to consider, beyond changes of energy, the detailed motion of the body in question.

The point of these remarks is to bring out the obvious point that in a subject matter as well-structured as physics, there will necessarily be a whole web of connections and relationships between different topics or between different questions. These relationships may operate at various levels: at the high level that all the four questions ultimately invoke a principle of conservation (a fact concealed in the first two), or at the lower level that both the first two concern uniform fields. A good banking system would attach at least some such information to items.

What would a simple natural description of the content of these items look like? A teacher might tell a class that they were about:

Q7   Gravitational potential in a uniform field
Q8   Electrical force in a uniform field
Q9   Potential energy in a uniform gravitational field
Q10 Acceleration in a uniform gravitational field.

The descriptions might be at a lower level of generality, for example describing Q9 and Q10 as concerning a car rolling down a hill, leaving the connection with gravity to be inferred. They might, though not very probably, be at a higher level, describing all as to do with conservative fields. The lower the level of description, the more is left to be filled in using knowledge of the subject.

The aim of the network is to give such items descriptions which are

(a)   reasonably compact
(b)   reasonably natural (i.e. close to a teacher's own
        description)
(c)   fairly close to the detail of the item
(d)   able to imply through the network important connections
        with related items.

The descriptions of content given to the four items in Figure 3.8.1 by the network in Figure 3.8.2 are:

Q7   UNIFORM GRAVITATIONAL POTENTIAL
Q8   UNIFORM ELECTRIC FIELDSTRENGTH
Q9   TRAJECTORY KE PE
Q10   TRAJECTORY ACCELERATION

The descriptions of Q9, 10 could be extended, adding UNIFORM GRAVITATIONAL FORCE to each, if it was judged that the source of the force making the car run downhill ought to be included. The form of the network is deliberately such that descriptions can be added to or be curtailed, at the judgment of the user, in such cases of doubt.

Space does not permit, and the specialised nature of the subject matter inhibits, any extended discussion of other examples of items and their coding. Instead, one or two general issues raised by such examples will be illustrated.

The value of a network in implying features of items without these having to be coded is brought out by examples having to do with electric current. These can be very varied, with currents flowing steadily or varying in several ways through a number of different components. The descriptions can say simply such things as that the item concerns current decaying in a capacitor circuit, or flowing steadily in a network of resistors, and despite the surface of the descriptions having almost nothing in common, the deeper similarities are implied.

One general problem is knowing how delicately to develop the network. A good example is the area of stretching and breaking solids, where the items differ appreciably in the detail of the physics. It was decided, however, not to represent this detail in this case, on the grounds that the importance of the topic was not great enough to justify more than broad description in such terms as 'deformation' or 'fracture'.

The network also has to deal with more than just physics content, since some legitimate items are not essentially about physics, but are about related aspects of the subject, notably mathematics. Thus the network provides for items described as to do with (for example) straight line graphs, with or without any description of what the graph is about. Such graphs are used so widely that there is sense in their being 'about nothing', whilst in other cases - such as differential equations - which have very characteristic applications though actually being very general, it is harder to decide whether to give them a 'contentless' description. The network thus has to have some flexibility in this respect, and not force an either-or choice.

3.8.4 Data Management

At the outset, the computer system requires the network of Figure 3.8.2 which is input as a series of 'sentences' describing each BAR or BRA, for example:

    CONTENT = BAR (MATTER CHANGE FIELD)
    MATTER   = BAR (MACRO MICRO)

etc. The network is then used to interpret all subsequent codes input to describe items.

Codes for items can then be input. There is of course managerial data as well as content code, so that the first question in Figure 3.8.1 might be entered as:

    Q684 = Y78 F6 D4 KEY(A) MC UNIFORM GRAV POTENTIAL

Y78 refers to the year of use, of which there may be several; F6 to the facility of about 60%; D4 to the discrimination of about

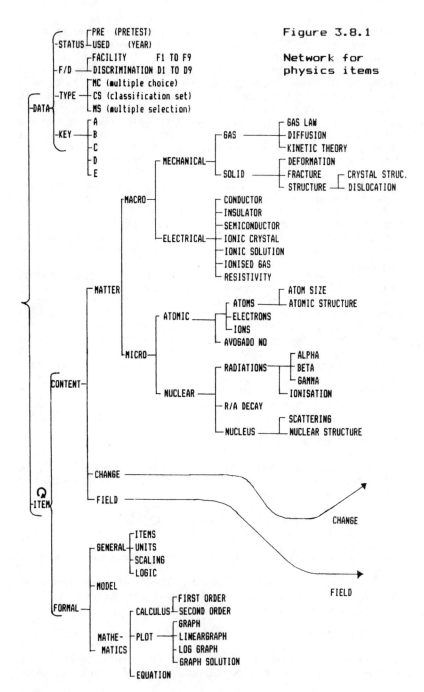

Figure 3.8.1

Network for physics items

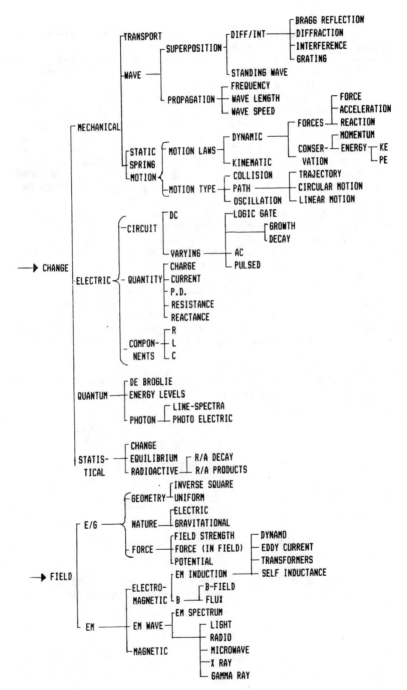

0.4, KEY(A) to the correct answer, and MC to the multiple choice format. The identifier of the item (Q684) is a name it gets when it enters the system from an item writer, ready for pretest, and under which it is filed.

Once items are input, the properties of the bank can be inspected, either to select items when constructing a paper or to locate features needed in new items so as to commission them economically.

The simplest form of questioning the bank is to request the number of items having a certain feature, or the names of items having a feature. Thus NUMBER (GRAV) given as a command prints out how many items include the term GRAV, while LIST (GRAV) gives the identifiers of all such items. A network term at any level of delicacy can be used, so that LIST (DISLOCATION) gives us all items about this small topic, while NUMBER (MATTER) finds how many items there are about all aspects of matter, including dislocations. Further, one can request compound properties. Thus LIST (MC AND (POTENTIAL OR FIELDSTRENGTH)) gets all multiple choice items which are either about potential or about fieldstrength. Again, terms in such an expression can be at any level of delicacy.

It may be that one wants to use a meaningful cluster of terms, such as all the classical (i.e. non-quantum) cases of waves or oscillations, and to do so frequently. One can define a new term CLASSWAVE, as DEF (CLASSWAVE) = (WAVE OR OSCILLATION) AND NOT (QUANTUM) and then list or get the number of all such questions.

Finally, the system allows for cross-tabulation with a command TAB which, given two lists of terms, produces a table showing the numbers of items having each paired combination of features. Table 3.8.1 shows an example.

	KINEMATICS	DYNAMICS
COLLISION	2	5
PATH	7	14
OSCILLATION	3	6

Table 3.8.1   Example of cross-tabulation using the content network

3.8.5 Discussion

Any practical item-banking system has to compare favourably to users with the system to which they are accustomed. While a case has been made in the foregoing description for such a system, its convenience is still a matter of doubt, and it has not passed the test of practical acceptance, in part because of the restricted availability of BARBARA but also because of the initial burdens of defining and learning to use the system.

It has to be said that the devising of the network to describe items is highly non-trivial. In common with 'expert systems' (see e.g. Michie 1979) developing such a network involves eliciting from examiners their perceptions of important features of content, and the relationships between such features.

The network of Figure 3.8.2 has been through many versions, the principal evolution having been towards greater flexibility of use. The network uses very few BRA's so imposing on the user very little by way of formal obligation to include terms from certain systems in the description of an item. Instead, the network is written as a single tree, with a recursive entry, so that the user picks a feature of an item, re-enters and picks another, and so on.

The network is not intended as an all-purpose one for any physics course, but is tailored for the Nuffield Advanced Level Physics course in particular. This is not to say that certain parts of it, perhaps much of it, could not be adapted for a network describing some similar course, though in fact its main structure, with the principal divisions MATTER, CHANGE, and FIELD reflects a view of the structure of the subject made explicit in the Nuffield teaching materials, and not generally shared by other A-level Physics courses. It might be counted as a disadvantage that the network as a whole is not readily transportable, or as an advantage that it does one job effectively instead of doing several less well.

The coding of items requires one to know the network fairly well, mainly so as to avoid using terms for features of questions they are not intended to describe.

One important decision was to keep codes as short as possible, partly to aid use of the system, and to exploit the property of a tree that delicate features inherit more global properties along branches of the tree, so that these properties did not have to go into codes.

An aim in choosing the network structure, and the mnemonic terms in it, was to have the codes look as far as possible much what a teacher might say about an item. After a time, this facilitates coding because commonly occurring clusters of terms in a code are remembered as a whole.

For the practical purposes of large Examination Boards, as they are in reality, the proposed system offers mainly promise, not proven performance. For research purposes, there seems - at least to the writer - a clear case for considering dealing with content of test items in some such way as proposed.

Note Views expressed are not necessarily those of the Oxford and Cambridge Examination Board or of the Nuffield Project.

3.9 LANGUAGE DEVELOPMENT AND THE LANGUAGE OF CONTROL

by Martin Monk and Jon Ogborn

3.9.1 Introduction

In this example, two studies are reported second hand, the first (Halliday 1975) being a study of early language development in one child, and the second (Turner 1973) an investigation of the language of control for children aged five and seven. Space prevents presenting more than a sketch of both, but they are included as instances of the use of networks in fields other than education, namely linguistics and socio-linguistics.

3.9.2 Development

Halliday (1975) collected continuous data on the developing language of one child (Nigel) from the age of nine months to eighteen months. Being in daily contact with the child, he collected a large corpus of material. Every six weeks, Halliday interpreted the corpus into a description of the child's language system at that stage, so producing a series of grammars of the child's language at these intervals. The grammars take the form of networks, which change in content and in structure over time.

The title of the study - 'Learning how to mean' - reveals Halliday's linguistic orientation, towards studying language as a meaning system in a social context. He takes a functional view of language, distinguishing in his other work (see Kress 1976, Halliday 1978) three major kinds of function of adult language: communication, interpersonal interaction, and (internal to language) the structuring, cohesive function. His interest in studying Nigel lies primarily in seeing how such functions might develop.

Whereas in adult language, functions of all three kinds are served at once by every utterance, Halliday maintains that for the young child each utterance has essentially one use. At nine months, Nigel had four small sets of utterances, serving respectively the functions of demand (gloss: 'give me'), command (gloss: 'do that'), interaction (gloss: 'nice to see you') and the personal (interest, niceness). The grammar thus consisted of sound-meaning pairs, with structure at first developing through more delicate differentiation of meanings and addition of new meanings. (For example, a meaning which could be glossed as 'give me' splitting into something specific - 'give me my toy bird' - and the more general 'give me that' idea).

Later, further functions developed: the heuristic, imaginative, and last, the informative. Notice that before Nigel's language - and so in Halliday's view what he could mean - included the informative function, he could not ask questions, lacking the idea that one can talk to tell people things.

We will present here just the development Halliday traces in one function, the interactional. At nine to 10.5 months Nigel's interactional repertoire had just three meanings, each with its own unique expression, as shown in Figure 3.9.1. He initiated or responded to interaction, the first being either a normal welcome or one showing some impatience.

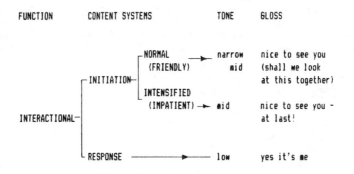

Figure 3.9.1   NL 1 Nigel 0:9 — 0:10.5

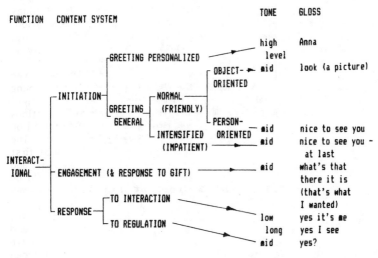

Figure 3.9.2   NL 2 Nigel 0:10.5 — 1:0

Analysis of Qualitative Data

Six weeks later, at 10.5 months to 1 year, the repertoire had
expanded to seven meanings, as in Figure 3.9.2. The previous normal
initiation of interaction had developed more delicate options of a
personalised greeting ('Anna') and a general one, the latter
containing the former impatient greeting as an option in systems also
containing a new distinction, of object versus person oriented
interaction ('look, a picture' versus 'shall we look at this').
Response to interaction is now divided into response to interaction
and to regulation: his language and his meanings respond to how
others behave; to what they mean. Further, a third kind of
interactional meaning has been added, that of engagement, but for the
moment as a single extra meaning with its own single expression.

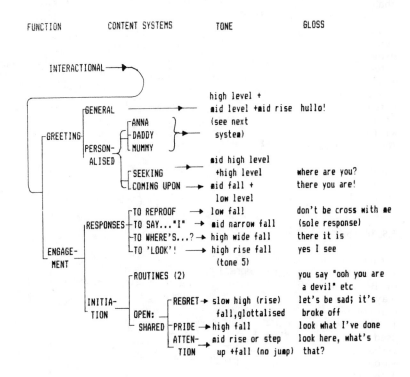

Figure 3.9.3   Nl 6 Nigel at 1:4.5 — 1:6

Figure 3.9.3 goes forward to the age 16.5 to 18 months, by which time the meaning system in the interactional function has become more elaborate, has reshaped itself, and has developed its first departure from the 'one meaning-one sound' principle of Nigel's early grammars. This last development appears in Figure 3.9.3 as the bracket following personalised greetings, for which Nigel has hit on the adult device of doing two things at once, here using a name to address a person and an intonation to mean the nature of the greeting (looking for someone or happening on them).

Halliday makes the point that it is here, with this structural change, that Nigel first truly has a language, in the sense of something more than specific sounds associated with specific functions, the latter being a structure more like that of birdsong than of English or French.

Fascinating though we find it, it is not for us to comment on the linguistic value of Halliday's work (it is controversial, and differs considerably from most other work in language development). As an exploitation of the network notation, however, it holds a special interest for our present purposes, which is worth discussing. One might suppose that networks are necessarily ill-adapted to describing change, since their very nature is to set out a structure of co-existing possibilities. What Halliday does is to follow change by producing a sequence of networks, each something like a snapshot. As with photographs of a child at different ages, one is led to compare the pictures and ask questions about how one changes into the next. Thus the networks provide material for analysis at two levels: the nature of each and the nature of their progression. Chapter 6 gives some further discussion of the representation of change using networks.

3.9.3 The Language of Control

Turner's (1973) work was influenced by Halliday, but was primarily sociological, being done with Bernstein and being directed in approach by Bernstein's theories of cultural transmission (in which language plays a central role). Turner looked at stories five and seven year old children told when given picture cards showing scenes in an incident of some boys playing with a ball and breaking a window. He used networks to map options in the system of meanings associated with verbal control, derived from what the children said the aggrieved window owner might say to the ball-players in order to restrain or deter them.

Bernstein's theory gives a special importance to role systems in the family seen as producing particular sets of preferred orientations to meanings (his term is code). In the domain of control, Bernstein is led to distinguish imperative and positional control systems, the distinction deriving from the posited nature of different role systems. Turner took this dichotomy, and developed it to more delicate levels, so as to be able to characterise what the children said and place their words in relation to the main distinction.

Figure 3.9.4 shows the first part of this development. Figure 3.9.5 shows how one term, threat, is elaborated.

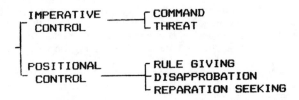

Figure 3.9.4   Control systems

Turner's problem was not, of course, to analyse the linguistic structure of the threats (or other control devices) offered, but to place them with respect to their different social meanings, and so it is terms descriptive of social relations that appear in the network: Examples of threats, indicating which options of the network they are taken to select, are:

I'll get you in prison	(1,10)
I'm going to give you a smack	(2,10)
I'll tell the police	(3,10)
I'm going to tell your mum, I'll tell the lady	(4,10)
If you do that once more, I'll punch you. Next time	(2,5,7)
you come round here, I'm going to spank you	(2,5,7)
If you do that once more, I'm going to tell the police	(3,5,7)
If you do that again I'll go and tell your mum	(4,5,7)
If you don't go, I'll call the police	(3,6,7)
Don't do it again, 'cos you'll go in prison	(1,5,8)
Don't come back because I'd give you a spank	(2,5,8)
Never do that again or you'll get smacked	(2,5,9)
Go on, go on or I'll get a stick and whack you	(2,6,9)
You come back or I'll tell a policeman	(3,6,9)
You pay for this, boys, or I take you to the police	(3,6,9)
You mustn't do that or else he'll go and tell their mother	(4,6,9)
You dare play football here again. You dare do this again	(11)
Don't you dare break that window again. Don't you dare do that again	(11)
You wait. Just wait. Wait until you come back.	(12)

Deriving from Bernstein, Turner's hypothesis was that both working and middle class children would select options from both positional and imperative modes, but that working class children would more often select the imperative mode and middle class children the positional (disapprobation and rule-giving). A more specific hypothesis was that

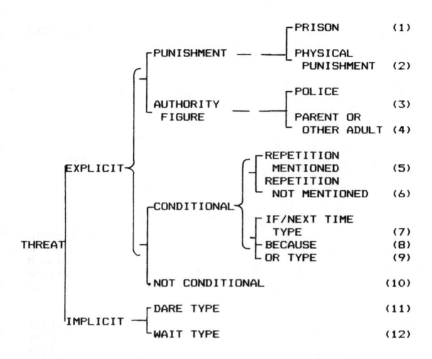

Figure 3.9.5   Network for THREAT

working class children would more often be less explicit in reference to the transgression. From an analysis of the coded transcripts, Turner found that more working class children did indeed mention control by means of threats, and he argues that this is one of the main ways in which imperative control is realised.   An interesting further result was that more working class children at the younger ages mentioned the grammatically complex conditional threat, reinforcing the view that 'code' in Bernstein's sense has to do not with grammatical richness or poverty, but with differential attention to kinds of meanings in interpersonal role relationships.

3.9.4 General Remarks

Halliday uses networks to show changing structures; Turner as coding frames. Both are theory laden, in Turner's case very explicitly so. Halliday's networks start from his basic structural-functional view of language, but although the theory does not tell him just what functions to expect a young child to have but (except in a very general way) it does tell him to look for functions.

PART II

LEATHER

PART THREE

LEARNING TO USE NETWORKS

Chapter 4

PRACTICALITIES AND ADVICE

This chapter is intended to help you start using networks yourself. At the outset it has to be said that a network cannot do the work for you: only you can produce the ideas that go into it. As the analyst you will still have to struggle with the evolution of your ideas, just as with any other data analysis technique.

4.1 STRUGGLE VERSUS PLOD

Most of the contributors in Chapter 3 emphasise the effort involved in developing a network. They are right to do so. Looking at a finished or even half finished network, it is difficult to imagine how what seem to be relatively obvious distinctions, combining in straight-forward ways, could have been so hard to arrive at. Try the exercises in Chapter 5 to experience something of this effect.

There are several reasons why network writing is hard if rewarding work. One reason is that the notation offers nothing but the barest essentials: choice, aspect, condition. It says nothing about what to say. Faced with data, even the simplest, one can think of many ways to begin a description, but one can not easily foresee how, when developed into a network, such descriptions will run out of steam, conflict with or repeat one another, or even simply come to seem superficial or feeble. The responsibility of going on to complete the network is a hard one to meet.

It is rarely possible to sit down and write a completely satisfactory network at one sitting. Sometimes a network may be developed over the course of a week; it is not unknown for it to take over six months. It is not uncommon to abandon up to a dozen failed attempts as confusions and contradictions become clearer. The struggle, however, is worthwhile as, step by step, one comes to clarify ideas and to know the data inside out. Don't give up too soon.

Networks can be seen as an aid in helping display categories and their connections, able to be used to communicate ideas in a compact and succinct way, and one of the best ways to evaluate one's progress is to show the network to a friend and try to explain exactly what the data is about and how the network is supposed to capture its essential features. It is not uncommon for a network presented to colleagues for discussion to pass rapidly from hopeful prospect to latest reject just because of the clear way a network sets out a scheme for criticism. After such a presentation one often finds one can approach the problem afresh perhaps in a different way with different categories. So don't plod on with an unsatisfactory network: throw it away and start again with the benefit of hindsight.

4.2 WHERE TO START

Faced with a large number of transcripts, a large number of stories or even just single comments, it is difficult to know what to put down on that clean sheet of blank paper. Working with all the data means that you have to keep a large number of subtle distinctions in your head. So make it easier by cutting the data down into smaller batches. Obviously the number in a batch will vary, but if all the data is too much and one single transcript or protocol is too few, perhaps ten is about right.

Another useful strategy is to begin with the easy bits of the network. There are usually some obvious and simple things one wants to say about the data, so make a start there. It is best not to try to be subtle or clever, but just to get going with something straightforward.

There is often a strong temptation to start a network with a small set of categories derived from some general theory. So, because the network seems to read from left to right one is tempted to start at the left-hand side of the page with such gross categories, dividing them more finely in moving towards the right-hand side. This does not always turn out to be the best thing to do: in fact starting from the right-hand side of the page may be best. This is simply because the right-hand side, at the terminals, is going to be closer to the actual data that you are trying to represent.

The goal is to produce a network which can code the data. It may be helpful to short-circuit this final stage, and to write informal summaries of the data, as if you could code it, well before you can do so. A sort of telegraphic resume of the data is what is needed: something like what a code would be, a kind of proto-code. Such summaries have the advantage of making the data physically more manageable, so that with care it is possible to reduce several pages of transcript to just a single side of informal summary. Working through a batch of data, try to use the same words consistently in the 'telegrams'. This will mean ignoring for the moment some of the more subtle shades of meaning that give the individual transcripts their life and originality. At a later stage you can decide if you want to revive those shades of meaning by developing the network further. From these telegrams a start can now be made on developing the potential terminals for the network. An advantage of this method of working is that it is easier to keep control on faithful representation of the data. A disadvantage is that it is easy to lose sight of the very important distinctions between data, codes and network terms. This is discussed more fully in Section 6.3.3.

4.3 CHART YOUR CHOICES AND CHANGES

Developing a network means making all sorts of decisions. In particular, as items of data are tentatively allowed to be described by some set of terms, one builds up reasons for deciding when a term fits and when not. It is not sensible to try to memorise such reasons, and much better to record them, so that there is less tendency for terms to shift or slide in meaning, as you use them on further data. Terms mean what you decided they meant, not what the word used seems to mean, nor what you can stretch terms to mean - unless you now want to change the previous decision.

One useful kind of record, especially for terminals, is to list a key word or phrase from each item of data which is currently counted as described by that terminal. It then remains clear that the terminal means 'what this list has in common'.

It is important both to be able to change a network easily, and to be able to remember what the change was and why it was made. Pencil and a good india rubber are better tools than pen and ink, especially in the early stages when there are frequent additions, deletions and changes of structure. But it is vital to record reasons for changes to the network, since these reasons are a diagnosis of what was wrong and how that is supposed to be now avoided. It is little use to be told that a network doesn't work, without being told why not.

For this purpose, it is especially valuable to have kept all previous attempts at networks. So, after working on a draft, date it and write on it comments about its current state. Keep the various versions in a file and look through the file from time to time, both to recover previous ideas and to check that the network is actually getting better.

4.4 FILLING IN THE MIDDLE

Do not be in too much of a hurry to write down single terms as labels for categories. In developing ideas that will fill out the middle regions of the network, first ideas are often loose. Rather than tightening the definition of the terms prematurely it is useful to put down a phrase or several words.

A watch should be kept for those seductive words that appear to capture potted meanings and simultaneously carry an air of respectability. Words such as 'neurotic', 'complex', 'role', 'social' and 'elaborated' have passed into usage, often with little or no regard for their precise original sense. Their use needs more than the usual discretion and care. Try replacing them with less respectworthy synonyms to see if the result looks equally valuable. More generally, it is often difficult to communicate the meanings in a network if the terms carry very strong unintended associations.

Several words are often better than one arbitrarily chosen term, so as to avoid this 'halo of meaning' effect.

It is a useful idea to try to attach some form of term, no matter how loose or long-winded, at each and every place in the network. That is, every BAR and BRA gets some kind of name. Doing this makes it less likely that you will assemble heterogeneous terms together, either as a set of distinctions that are merely different but not related, or as a set of simultaneous aspects which have no coherence. The name for each BAR or BRA should say what it is about, and will guide future development of more delicate systems.

Working with soft pencil and rubber you can afford to move terms about and try out different structures of BARs and BRAs with the same set of terms. Doing this helps to settle the relative status with respect to delicacy of different systems. Again it is important to keep a note of what you have tried and the reasons for keeping or rejecting a particular configuration.

When several terms make repeated appearances as neighbours in a network, it is time to stop and decide whether to continue with that particular arrangement of the terms. It might be that you need a BRA somewhere earlier in the network, at a grosser level of delicacy, to take care of the repetitions.

With the BAR notation alone it is simply tree diagrams that are being constructed and the principal problem is keeping a watch on the development of the paradigms to more delicate levels. With the BRA notation there is the added problem of keeping parallel treelike branches of the network in step. When you have developed a bit of the network to the right of any BRA it is worthwhile checking that the categories at any given level of delicacy are of the same sort of gross distinction. This is best achieved by simply keeping terms in vertical columns so that delicacy can be checked by running an eye up columns. Where there is uncertainty about the appropriateness of any level of delicacy for a given set of terms, make use of the vertical columns to place those that you feel fairly confident about and tentatively string out others across the remaining vertical columns for future checking.

In some of the examples reference is made to 'managerial' 'strategic', and 'content' or 'descriptive' aspects of the network. These distinctions are not part of the formal language of networks that was set out in Chapter 2. They do however provide useful ways of thinking about doing different sorts of jobs with terms as you construct networks. In fact we have tended to find ourselves talking about regions within networks that do different jobs of work. So, the descriptive region contains terms that deal with the content of the data proper, whilst managerial regions have terms that reflect the organisation of the data. Thus, for example, for the purpose of looking at classroom interaction children could be classified managerially according to their sex, the clique they are in, and their social class background. The managerial section of the network can label subjects in many such ways. The strategic section of the network is very different: here the analyst is faced with creating a scheme that will structure the analysis. Such schemes are not all self-evident. For instance, in Example 3.1 about students' reactions to learning it was decided to break down lengthy stories into clauses, with each clause analysed in terms of a topic and a comment about the topic. Topics and comments could then be developed to deal with the data itself.

This was the strategic decision in that case. It is not always straightforward to decide which terms in any network should actually be thought about in each of these three ways. However, even though no decision is actually needed, or may even be taken, thinking along these lines does help to disentangle some potential confusions.

4.5 REVIEWING THE FIRST ATTEMPT

As we said earlier, one of the best ways of reviewing your network is to go off and try to explain it to your colleagues. There are however some preliminary checks which you can make first.

The simplest and most straightforward is on the notational aspects of the network. Have you actually got BARs and BRAs respectively where you intended them to be? A second check is to make sure that each of the BARs and BRAs can be given a term to label the system as well as the terms of the system themselves. Now write out each and every paradigm that the network will allow. Ask yourself if there is anything missing or anything that is patently ridiculous which should not be allowed. Finding such problems is not difficult, but deciding what should be done about them is not always so easy. Issues about consistency in networks are discussed in more detail in Chapter 8 (Section 8.2.2).

In looking at the paradigms of your network ask if they actually come close to bringing out the sorts of points that you feel are important. Sometimes it is easy to slide into a pre-occupation with the surface detail of qualitative data at the cost of developing the substantive analysis. Ask yourself if this has happened. Also ask yourself if the level of analysis - the size of the unit that it has attempted to describe - is right. This aspect of rank is discussed in more detail in Section 6.2.1 of Chapter 6.

When the approach to a problem under investigation is informed through some pre-given theoretical framework it is worth looking carefully at the way in which ideas from that framework have been introduced in the use of terms, the distinctions of the BARs and BRAs, or the distribution of managerial, strategic and descriptive regions. Does the network actually represent in any way that pre-given orientation? If it does (as one would hope) exactly how is that achieved?

At this stage of checking it is useful to run an eye along the branches of the network from the left-most terms down through the levels of delicacy to the right-hand terminals, looking to see if there has been any loss of focus en route. A loss of focus can occur when inadvertently the systems at any BAR or BRA are followed by others related to it more by association of words than by genuine cases of choice, aspect or condition.

4.6   DATA TO NETWORK – NETWORK TO DATA

Just as your network should be developed with regard to your data so a return to the data must be made in order to evaluate the network. A systematic approach to this can speed things up in the long run, even though it may appear to be somewhat tedious at first.

Each of the paradigms that had previously been written out in the earlier check on the network must now be taken in turn and an instance of that paradigm looked for in the data set being dealt with. Where instances are to be found, how well does the paradigm capture what you may have previously seen as being the essential flavour of that bit of data? Where instances cannot be found the problem is more subtle. Thought needs to be given to what the network is attempting to represent and as to whether or not the absence of instances is a fault or an interesting fact. Problems of the completeness of a network are discussed at greater length in Chapter 8 (Section 8.2.1).

4.7   CODING PROBLEMS

Now is the time to refer back to all the notes made as the network developed. With a complete record one should be in a strong position to give firm reasons as to why some parts of the data instance one paradigm and other parts another. These reasons are now criteria for classifying the data. Armed with these an attempt should be made to code a further batch of data or its telegraphic summaries. This is a critical time to find out whether you have a viable network or not. If your network crashes because it fails to describe some important feature of the new data, then it may be possible to add that feature in. If you do find yourself doing this then you are essentially back at Section 4.3 of this chapter and there is still some way to go, charting your changes, continuing to fill in the middle, reviewing that attempt, and working from network to data and data to network, so that you may once again try out a new set of coding rules developed from your notes.

Should you have repeated this cycle of working to your own satisfaction then you might now consider the level of delicacy to which the network should be appropriately developed. Perhaps you are going to be happy with stopping at the terminals you initially worked on. On the other hand you may feel that some change is needed. Either the network can be pruned back, or alternatively be extended. In the first case there will be a loss in the subtlety of description but it may become more reliable. In the second it is possible to extend the delicacy of the network so as to get a closer correspondence with the data if you can really recognise the finer distinctions. Which to do depends primarily on the point of the whole analysis; something that should naturally have informed every stage of the work.

Chapter 5

EXERCISES IN WRITING NETWORKS

The exercises in this chapter are intended to help the new user of networks to become familiar with the network notation described in Chapter 2.   Each exercise is provided with an answer, or a possible answer, which discusses briefly some of the difficulties of that exercise.   Since exercises have been chosen to reveal various problems, the most profitable use of the answers will be as a basis for a critical comparison with the possiblities suggested to the reader in doing the exercises.

The data used for exercises is taken from areas that are likely to be well known to the reader, so that commonsense knowledge should be enough.   Such a choice is deliberate, since we did not want difficulties of knowing a body of data to be an obstacle to learning to write and think about networks.   It seemed more important here for the reader to see what options the notation makes available, and to experiment or even play with them so as to become more at ease with the whole system.

The exercises have been constructed to serve a number of purposes.   Exercises 1 to 5 are intended to get the user into the habit of reading networks, of looking at paradigms generated by a network, or writing codes for and finding instances of paradigms, and constructing networks from paradigms.   Exercises 6 and 7 involve translating networks to and from contingency tables.   Examples 8 a-d provide very simple data for the construction of networks.

Exercises 9 to 15 are likely to prove a little more difficult. In exercises 9 and 10 the reader is required to take a more critical stance, either in considering whether the development of a set of given categories makes good sense, or in thinking about the implications of alternative notations for a set of categories. Exercises 11 and 12 involve using more sophisticated data in network construction.   Lastly, exercises 13, 14 and 15 raise issues such as the purpose of the analysis, and the choice of categories in function of this purpose.

Despite our having provided answers the user will discover that there are no 'right' answers.   Any network necessarily reflects the ideas, pre-occupations and perceptions of the analyst.

5.1 EXERCISES

Exercise 1

Write out the distinctions made in the network in Figure 5.1 as prose.

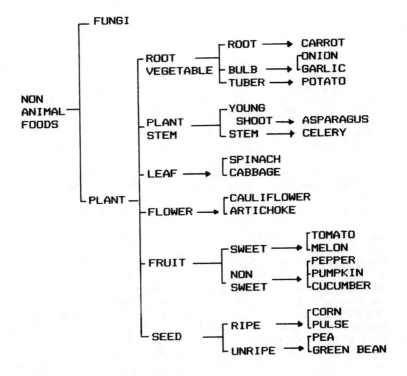

Figure 5.1   Non-animal foods

Exercise 2

In Figure 5.2 a TUBA is an instance of the paradigm WIND BASS whereas a TRIANGLE is an instance of the paradigm PERCUSSION UPPER. Look at the other paradigms and see if you can find at least one instance of each.

Discuss why it is difficult to assimilate a piano to this network.

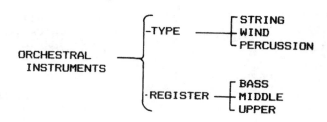

Figure 5.2   Orchestra

Exercise 3

The network in Figure 5.3 was written to describe what a mother is doing when she regulates the behaviour of a child. Or rather, it shows what she CAN do in as much as it states the possibilities that are open to her. The categories PERSONAL, POSITIONAL, OBJECT-ORIENTED and PERSON-ORIENTED are taken from Basil Bernstein (1973). They deal with family role systems and procedures of social control.

One example of the extended code for a paradigm of the network is:

    CONTROL (PERSONAL (THREAT(CONDITIONAL)))
    ORIENTATION (OBJECT ORIENTED)

Write out similar extended codes for at least three of the other paradigms.

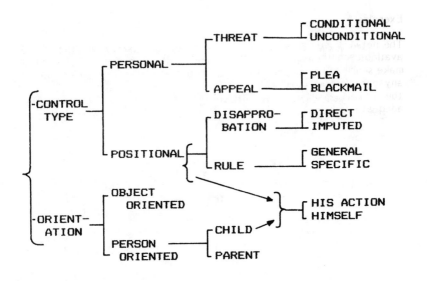

Figure 5.3   Regulation of child behaviour

Exercise 4

The (abstract) network in Figure 5.4 generates the paradigms: AC, AD, BC, BD.
    Draw networks which generate all (and only) the lists 1 and 2 and attempt to draw a network for list 3.

Figure 5.4   Abstract network

LIST 1	LIST 2	LIST 3
A	AC	AC
BC	AD	ADF
BE	BC	ADG
CD	BD	AEF
CE	EC	AEG
	EH	BC
	FG	BDF
	FH	BDG
		BEF
		BEG

Exercise 5

The network in Figure 5.5 is a first attempt to describe the journals available on the market. Work out all the paradigms and see which make sense and which do not. Inspect the network to see in what way any paradigms thought to be non-sensical relate to the structure of the network. Attempt to modify the network so that they are given an adequate description.

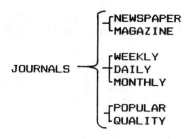

Figure 5.5   Descriptions of journals

Exercise 6

Express the network in Figure 5.6 as a contingency table.

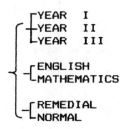

Figure 5.6   Children in various
school groupings

125

Exercise 7

Science undergraduates in an English university were interviewed and were asked to tell a story about a time when learning was either particularly good or particularly bad. The contingency table 5.1 summarises the total number of different kinds of stories told. Re-express this table as a network.

	FIRST YEAR		SECOND YEAR		THIRD YEAR		
	GOOD STORIES	BAD STORIES	GOOD STORIES	BAD STORIES	GOOD STORIES	BAD STORIES	TOTAL
LECTURES							
LABORA- TORIES							
TUTORIALS							
EXAMINA- TIONS							
INDIVIDUAL STUDY							
TOTAL							

Table 5.1   Good and bad stories about learning

Exercise 8

Part (a)   The Venn diagram Figure 5.7 was drawn by a group of children to show how they had sorted out a pile of toys. Represent the Venn diagram in the form of a network.

Figure 5.7   Animals

Part (b)   Some young children were given a set of different coloured geometrical shapes and were asked to sort them out by 'putting together the things that go well together'.   The schema in table 5.2 shows how one group of children did this.   Draw a network to represent this classification.

BOX ONE

RED AND BLUE
TRIANGLES, SQUARES
AND RECTANGLES

BOX TWO

RED AND BLUE
ELLIPSES AND
CIRCLES

Table 5.2   Classification of
geometrical shapes

Part (c)   Teachers were asked to make a statement about every child in their tutorial group saying how good or bad a child was both in academic performance and classroom behaviour.   Draw the beginnings of a network that will represent the situation.

Part (d)   Represent the following distinctions in the form of a network.

"When talking about schools in England we need to ask the three following basic questions.   What type of school is it, that is, does it belong to the private or public sector?   Is it mixed or not?   What size of school is in question: relatively small up to about 400; medium up to about 1400; or large above 1400?".

Exercise 9

The two networks in Figure 5.8 have just been started.   Try to extend
them to further levels of delicacy.   If necessary reformulate a
distinction already shown.

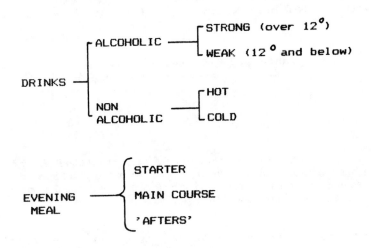

Figure 5.8   Networks for drink and meals

Exercise 10

Discuss the differences and similarities between the ways the three networks in Figure 5.9 handle the same distinctions. The intention of the distinctions is to describe a teacher's behaviour. A first distinction can be made between COGNITIVE and AFFECTIVE. This refers either to how the teacher appears intellectually, when carrying out his job; or to how he appears non-academically, his personal emotional side. A second distinction is between INTERPERSONAL and INDIVIDUAL. This, in turn, refers to how he is seen when he is interacting with other people, mainly students, or how he is when he is on his own.

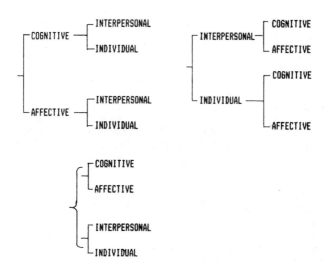

Figure 5.9   Teacher's behaviour

Exercise 11

Here are some possible forms of address used in letters:

> Sirs
> Dear Sir
> Dear Mr. Smith
> Dear John
> Darling

Attempt a tree network to describe the grading of intimacy they express.   Include other forms of address.

Exercise 12

The list below gives a collection of greetings used in middle class British English.   Attempt to draw a network to represent them.

> Hullo
> Goodbye
> Good morning *
> Good afternoon *
> Good night
> How do you do?
> Good evening
> Bye Bye

(* The items "good morning" and "good afternoon" each need to be treated as two items, because, depending on the intonation, they can be used on parting or meeting.)

Exercise 13

Figure 5.10 shows a first attempt to write a network for the furniture and fittings of a home.

Should items such as televisions and portable radios be included in this classification and, if so, where do they go? Think of an alternative way of classifying this data particularly when a more exhaustive list of furniture and fittings is drawn up. Consider the purposes of alternative networks.

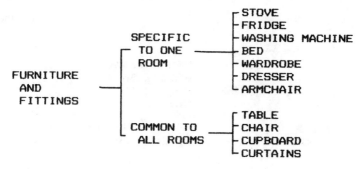

Figure 5.10 Furniture and fittings

Exercise 14

Teachers and parents were asked about what sorts of punishments they threatened when dealing with a difficult child. A list of those mentioned includes:

Stopping pocket money
Slapping
Detention
Being sarcastic
Discussing with the child
Writing lines
Confiscation of item
Caning
Telling-off
Stopping watching TV
Using the slipper
No pudding
Child's own choice of punishment

Draw a network to show the different types of meanings these punishments might have to a child. Attempt also to make the list more exhaustive by suggesting further punishments and see if these fit within your network, or whether the network needs reshaping.

Exercise 15

Figure 5.11 is a first attempt at a network for various modes of communication. Criticise the network as a useful description of such modes.

Suppose the first distinctions were LEARNING and ENTERTAINMENT: how should the rest of the network be changed? Try other distinctions such as DIRECT and INDIRECT and see what sorts of network you can develop.

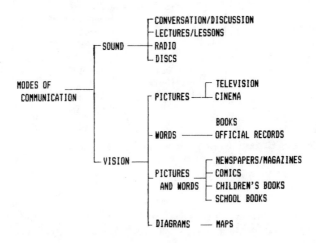

Figure 5.11   Modes of communications

5.2 ANSWERS

Answer to Exercise 1

This exercise is fairly straightforward due to the fact that there are no co-selections that need to be borne in mind. The network is essentially a tree structure. It was based on the following, from Larousse Gastronomique.

> "Vegetable foods can be divided into two major divisions: these are fungi and the edible parts of plants. The edible parts of plants can be further categorised as being either roots, plants, stems, leaves, flowers, fruit or seeds. In turn, roots can be further subdivided into roots proper, bulbs and tubers etc., etc.".

Answer to Exercise 2

In answering the first part of this question there are two jobs that need to be done. The first is to work out from the network what the co-selections are that will make up the various paradigms. Altogether this network allows for the expression of nine paradigms; string bass, string middle, string upper, wind bass, wind middle, wind upper, and percussion bass, percussion middle and percussion upper. The second job is to find instances of these paradigms. For the string section of a European concert orchestra the string bass, string middle and string upper paradigms could be instanced by double bass, viola and violin, respectively.

The second part of the question can be dealt with at two levels. The first level is simply to say that the problem with a piano is that it has struck strings, so that it is a 'string percussion' instrument, and that it also has a register which cuts across the three ranges bass, middle and upper. At a second level of answer it would be possible to try and reformulate the network so that one could assimilate the piano into some newly developed network. (The network could be made to account for a more comprehensive field of data if you bear in mind the other instruments that sometimes appear on the contemporary concert platform, such as synthesizers).

Answer to Exercise 3

The example of the long hand code for the paradigm given in the exercise is arrived at by working along the options presented by the uppermost term at each of the nodes, after CONTROL TYPE and ORIENTATION. Another example would be:

CONTROL (THREAT(PERSONAL(UNCONDITIONAL)))
ORIENTATION(OBJECT ORIENTED)

Analysis of Qualitative Data

where only the terminal at the least delicate level has been changed. Selecting other options at an earlier stage might give the paradigm:

CONTROL(PERSONAL(APPEAL(BLACKMAIL)))
ORIENTATION(PERSON ORIENTED(PARENT))

When we come to deal with POSITIONAL CONTROL there is a choice to be made between DISAPPROBATION and RULE if the ORIENTATION co-selection happens to be OBJECT-ORIENTED or PERSON ORIENTED (PARENT). If however the PERSON ORIENTATION happens to be that of the CHILD, then there is not only the choice between DISAPPROBATION and RULE to be made, but there is also a choice between HIS ACTIONS and HIMSELF to be made.

We hope that you had a go at trying to select a paradigm which involved these entry conditions. If you didn't, then we advise you to try.

Answer to Exercise 4

Figure 5.12 gives networks for Lists 1, 2 and 3.

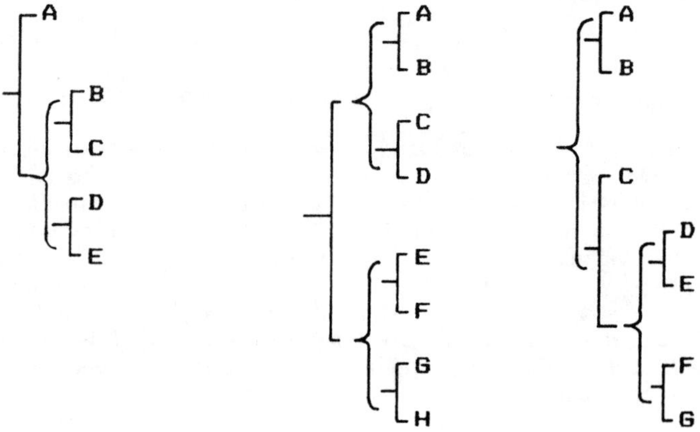

Figure 5.12   Networks for Lists 1,2 and 3

Answer to Exercise 5

With the network as it stands in Figure 5.5 of exercise 5, there are 12 possible paradigms. Two of the paradigms MAGAZINE DAILY POPULAR and MAGAZINE DAILY QUALITY do not make sense as magazines by their nature are periodical and not daily publications. Bearing this in mind, it can be seen that the distinctions set out in Figure 5.5 are all at the same level of delicacy, whereas the distinctions related to time - DAILY, WEEKLY, MONTHLY - should, in fact, be a finer level of delicacy of the distinction NEWS-PAPER/MAGAZINE.

The network in Figure 5.13 has been written to take account of this modification. As a result of this the number of paradigms has been reduced to 10 (from the original 12). The descriptions now seem to be more adequate, but paradigms involving NEWSPAPER MONTHLY do raise the query of whether or not such journals exist.

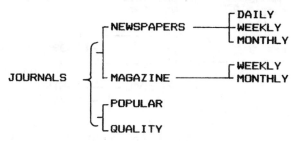

Figure 5.13   Revised network for JOURNALS

Answer to Exercise 6

The network (Figure 5.6) in exercise 6 can be re-expressed as the contingency table Table 5.3.

	YEAR I		YEAR II		YEAR III	
SUBJECT	REMEDIAL	NORMAL	REMEDIAL	NORMAL	REMEDIAL	NORMAL
ENGLISH						
MATHE-MATICS						
TOTAL						

Table 5.3   Children in various
                 school groupings

Analysis of Qualitative Data

Answer to Exercise 7

The contingency table (Table 5.1) in Exercise 7 can be re-expressed as the network in Figure 5.14.

This network though representing the contingency table in Exercise 7, introduces some distinctions which are not in the original table. These are those between different sizes of teaching groups, introduced at a level of delicacy above that of the types of class used in the table. Such terms correspond to one way of collapsing the original contingency table. You may be able to think of alternatives.

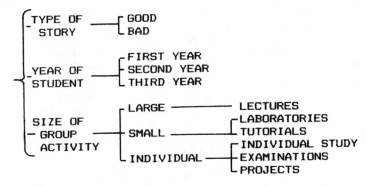

Figure 5.14   Network for good and bad stories
about learning at university

Answer to Exercise 8

Part (a): Figure 5.15 is simply a network representation of nested sets.

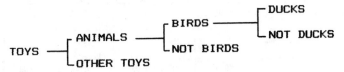

Figure 5.15   Network for toys

Part (b): Figure 5.16(a) is intended provocatively.   It is a reminder that, purely on the evidence mentioned, we have no way of knowing whether the children sorted by colours, or distinguished triangles from squares.

In fact, a descriptive network is more likely to look like Figure 5.16(b).   The two answers emphasise, albeit trivially, the importance of being sure whose point of view is represented.

136

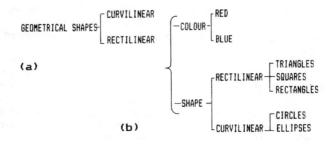

Figure 5.16   Alternative networks for
geometrical shapes

Part (c): Figure 5.17(a) shows the 'obvious' answer to Exercise 8(c).
It is not, however, the only one, nor necessarily the best.   Built
into it is the assumption that goodness and badness are of the same
qualitative kind, with reference to academic performance or classroom
behaviour.   Figure 5.17(b) shows the beginning of a possible
alternative scheme, which makes some attempt to spell out the
differences.

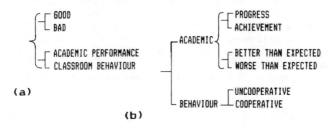

Figure 5.17   Different ways of representing
academic performance and classroom
behaviour

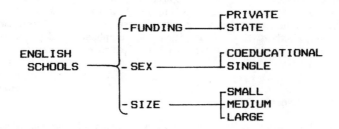

Figure 5.18   English schools

Part (d): Figure 5.18 shows an answer to Exercise 8(d), which though acceptable on the information given, could nevertheless be seen as trite. What ought to replace it would depend on the function of an actual analysis.

Answer to Exercise 9

The drinks network looks as though a good start has been made with some fairly sensible looking distinctions on the left hand side. But the distinction of HOT and COLD on the NON-ALCOHOLIC drinks leads one to think of HOT and COLD ALCOHOLIC drinks, such as punches and toddies, or whisky on the rocks and shandy with ice. It then becomes apparent that in order to be able to deal with this either HOT and COLD needs to be able to co-selected with STRONG, MEDIUM and WEAK ALCOHOLIC drinks, or, HOT and COLD needs to be taken out at this level of delicacy and put at the less delicate level of the distinction of ALCOHOLIC and NON-ALCOHOLIC, so that it may be co-selected with either. By thinking of other drinks, such as cocktails, a whole new dimension needs to be added in terms of a distinction between mixed and un-mixed drinks. And so it can go on, with every new drink that can be thought of requiring either some minor modification or being assimilable to the network.

The network on the evening meal looks fine, until you happen to think about what might be the case if you were to dine out at a Chinese restaurant, when some modifications might be required. The simplest modification is to re-title the whole network to being 'British middle-class evening meals', say, but although this is a neat solution, it does not help you practice your network building.

Answer to Exercise 10

The three networks shown in Figure 5.9 (a), (b), (c) are in some sense equivalent. However, the meanings they distinguish vary. In figure (c) the co-selection of COGNITIVE or AFFECTIVE and INTER-PERSONAL or INDIVIDUAL, implies that these two pairs of categories are of similar standing, appearing as they do at the same level of delicacy. In both Figures 5.9 (a) and (b), the fact that there are two levels of delicacy implies that the terms distinguished at the least delicate level are in some sense primary. The networks differ in which distinction is given that emphasis, a decision which can only be justified in terms of the purpose and nature of the analysis.

Answer to Exercise 11

One kind of solution for a network for forms of address is just a single bar as in Figure 5.19(a).

A better solution, expressing a more structured insight (right or wrong) into the differences, might progressively introduce more and more delicate distinctions perhaps as in Figure 19(b).

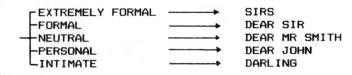

(a)

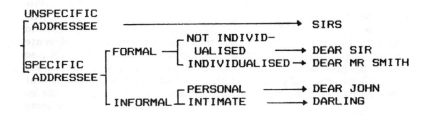

(b)

Figure 5.19 Networks for forms of address

Answer to Exercise 12

The network in Figure 5.20 (Halliday, 1973) is a possible way of organising the greetings listed in Exercise 12.

This network gives rise to ten paradigms, instances of which are:

Hail informal	Hullo
Hail formal	How do you do?
Hail time-bound morning	Good morning (rising intonation)
Hail time-bound afternoon	Good afternoon (rising intonation)
Hail time-bound evening	Good evening
Farewell informal	Bye Bye
Farewell formal	Goodbye
Farewell time-bound morning	Good morning (falling intonation)
Farewell time-bound afternoon	Good afternoon (falling intonation)
Farewell time-bound evening	Goodnight

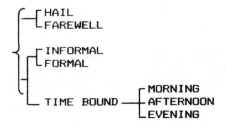

Figure 5.20   Network for greetings

Answer to Exercise 13

This exercise attempts to bring out that you may need a very different network according to the purpose of the analysis.   The one suggested in the exercise might be useful only to furniture removers.

Televisions and portable radios are just two sets of objects in a category that covers a range of devices, machines or gadgets.   Other such objects are, for example, video recorders, tape decks, Hoovers, irons, sewing machines.   We should also include in such a category objects such as fridges, washing machines and electric or gas cookers which had previously been categorised 'specific to one room' in our network in the exercise.   All these objects are usually fairly costly either to repair, when the guarantee is up, or to replace if broken or stolen.   If the purpose of a network were to consider the cost of maintenance of objects in the home such a category would be an important one.

A network with a different purpose would be to consider objects in   terms   of   their   function   within   the   furniture   and   fittings description.   There are several functions which can be classified as ESSENTIAL.   The first is to do with the care and preparation of food.   A second important function that objects have is to make people's everyday physical existence reasonable, for example chairs, tables, beds, lamps.   Storage is yet another very critical function.

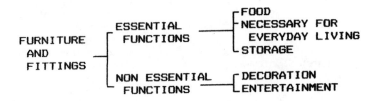

Figure 5.21   Function of furniture network

There are also objects whose function might be considered as NON ESSENTIAL but which are nevertheless a common part of every day furniture and fittings. A first function in this category would be to do with decoration and things such as curtains, carpets, cushions, pictures, etc. would be instances. A second function in this category would be to do with entertainment and within this would be included televisions, radios, tape decks etc. A beginning of a network along these lines might be as shown in Figure 5.21.

Answer to Exercise 14

The type of network to be drawn up for the punishments listed in Exercise 14 will depend a great deal on the age of child as well as probably the type of child. A fifteen year old child might make the three distinctions shown in Figure 5.22(a).

A seven year old might view the punishments in the manner described in Figure 5.22(b).

Compare your answer with someone else's and see what distinctions they have made. Consider whether the network you have drawn is really from the point of view of an adult and not a child.

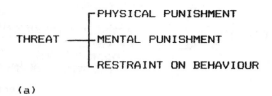

(a)

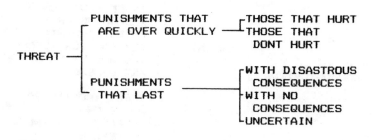

(b)

Figure 5.22   Different views of
punishment

Answer to Exercise 15

In the network for modes of communication the SOUND/VISION distinction does not hold up in such cases as TELEVISION and CINEMA where sound and vision are intricately linked. This is also the case for CONVERSATION/DISCUSSION and LECTURES/ LESSONS where the presence of the person provides an important visual aspect.

The simple network given in Figure 5.23(a) starts with the distinctions LEARNING and ENTERTAINMENT.

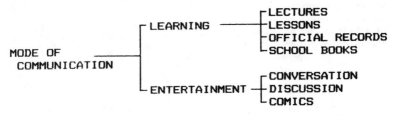

(a)

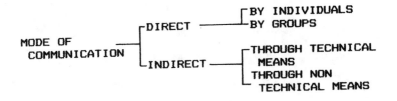

(b)

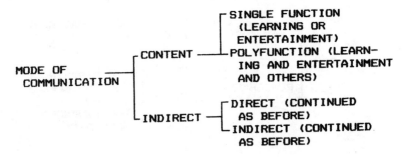

(c)

Figure 5.23   Various ways of representing
modes of communication

When we attempt to classify the other terms of the network in Exercise 15 we immediately run into difficulty as they can be used as a mode of communication for both learning and entertainment.

A network using the distinction DIRECT/INDIRECT might give us the beginning shown in Figure 5.23(b). Instances of the paradigm MODE OF COMMUNICATION (DIRECT (BY GROUPS)) are CONCERTS and PLAYS, and instances of the paradigm MODE OF COMMUNICATION (INDIRECT(THROUGH TECHNICAL MEANS)) are CINEMA, TELEVISION, RADIO.

This network has its limitations also in that it uses only two levels of delicacy. A possible way of getting a more comprehensive network would be to consider putting the two distinctions LEARNING/ENTERTAINMENT and DIRECT/INDIRECT on a BRA in the manner shown in Figure 5.23(c).

PART FOUR

GENERAL ISSUES

Chapter 6

WORKING WITH NETWORKS

This chapter, which begins a new section of the book concerned with issues and problems, looks forward to the wider implications of network notation and usage but also links back to previous chapters. Some of the definitions given in Chapter 2 are expanded and looked at critically; some of the practicalities and advice of Chapter 4 are taken further and developed in terms of instances in networks; and various points discussed in the examples in Chapter 3 are considered in relation to problems of manipulating existing networks or thinking of alternative ones. It also attempts to give the reader a more general view of networks and how they are or can be used in a variety of situations. The chapter falls into three main sections: the first, 6.1, looks at networks and where meaning is located within them; 6.2 discusses different kinds of problems data presents and how networks attempt to cope with them; and 6.3 considers what alternatives are available in handling the output of coded data.

6.1 MEANING AND STRUCTURE

Section 6.1.1 will look at the ways in which meaning can be expressed through a network or, more precisely, at what sorts of meaning the notation will allow to be represented. In Section 6.1.2 issues to do with how meaning is related to the structure or architecture of the network are considered.

6.1.1 Meanings in Networks

Where is it that meanings are represented in networks? How is it that the network says (or doesn't say) what the analyst has in mind? The answer, not surprisingly, depends upon the physical construction of the network itself. The meaning resides both in the terms, and in the BARs, BRAs and CONs, that is in the distinctions that the notation allows. There are three points to make about the location of meaning, to do with the terms themselves, their linkages to other terms at the same level of delicacy and their links to terms at prior

Figure 6.1   Meaning in terms of network

and subsequent levels of delicacy.   The points to be made here collect together a number of matters that were implicit in Chapter 2.
Certainly some meaning resides in the choice of terms.   As with any category scheme, words have to be used to communicate the nature of any given category.   The fact that one term rather than another is used, indicates that the analyst has power to communicate meaning through the network's terms themselves.   This may appear to be a rather trivial point, but for all that it is easily overlooked.   In Section 8.2.1 it will be examined in more detail from the point of view of what makes a 'better' network.
The loading of meaning onto terms is illustrated by the network in Figure 6.1 describing kinds of buildings.   It is the common usage associations of the terms in this system that allows the meaning to be immediately understood.   And the meanings that can be read encompass a whole range of features of buildings such as their size, usage, location etc., none of which are written in the network.
If the example on buildings is pursued from the point of view of creating a network containing an explicit typology of buildings, then it might look something like that shown in Figure 6.2.   A bungalow would now be coded as a DOMESTIC, ONE STOREY, COUNTRY building, whereas a skyscraper would be coded as a COMMERCIAL building over 20 STOREYS with a TOWN LOCATION.
What has happened here is that some of the taken for granted information that was previously stored in the terms skyscraper and bungalow, has been unpacked and layed out for inspection.   And this

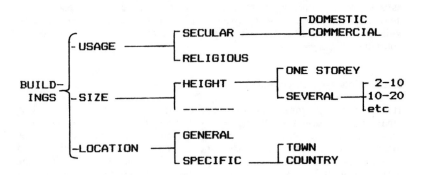

Figure 6.2 Typology of buildings network

has been achieved by paying attention to several co-occurring global features, usage, size and location.

At the same time, the meaning in a network resides, in part, in the distinctions of the notation. On a BAR one term is set in contrast with the other terms, and part of the meaning of any of the terms in the systems arises out of that set of contrasts. Similarly with a BRA, part of the meaning of any term is implied by its co-occurrence with the given set of other terms. Should any one of the terms be changed, the meaning of all the other terms becomes somewhat different, both for systems of BARs and co-occurrences with BRAs.

Example 3.2, on children's classification strategies for foodstuffs, usefully illustrates how the meaning resides both in the terms and the distinctions that the notation allows. In considering the context dependent part of Janet Holland's network Figure 3.2.1 the term FOOD ATTRIBUTES is present in response to the nature of the study itself. Meaning is conveyed to the reader in the choice of the words FOOD ATTRIBUTES, emphasising the particular area of the materials used in eliciting children's classification strategies. In addition meaning is also conveyed in the fact that this term stands as one in a system of four which includes PERCEPTUAL FEATURES, EVERYDAY USE and AMBIGUOUS/ IMPLICIT, which emphasises the context dependent nature of the reponses so classified.

In this example, as indeed with all others, part of the meaning is also carried through the prior term, which in this case is CONTEXT DEPENDENT, and in subsequent terms at more delicate levels, here the terms PREPARATION and STORAGE/SOURCE. The reader's understanding of the term FOOD ATTRIBUTES is informed by the use of both the prior and subsequent terms, as well as simply the term itself. The context dependence points us in the direction of a Bernsteinian framework, whilst the more delicate terms of PREPARATION and STORAGE/SOURCE pick out the attributes to which attention should be paid.

Meaning can be immediately got from the network by looking at it as a whole. It is not just the isolated terms alone, but also the distinctions and co-occurrences at any given level of delicacy, as well as the terms at prior and subsequent levels of delicacy, that contribute.

6.1.2 Changes of Structure - Changes of Meaning

It is important to be aware that relatively small changes in the structure of a network can produce rather radical changes in meaning. This problem will be discussed through an extended consideration of an example, that of one child's view of sums (Example 3.4). One part of Karen's view of the appearance of sums has to do with how sums are written down. This fragment of the network is repeated in Figure 6.3.

This network tells us that Karen sees the appearance of the constituents of sums as having to do with the SIGNS in the sums as

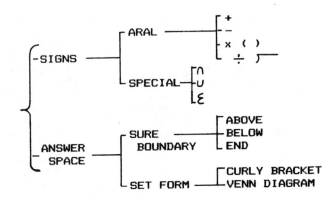

Figure 6.3   Part of network concerning Karen's
view of appearance of sums

well as something about the ANSWER SPACE.   Of the SIGNS
there are ARAL ones and SPECIAL ones, and the ANSWER
SPACES are also of two forms; those where the way in which the
sum is set out organises a space for where the answer should go, and
those where you draw VENN DIAGRAMS or put things in.

For this fragment of network alone there are some twenty-five
diffent paradigms, which include the possibility of Venn diagram
answers to sums in simple arithmetic.   Contrast this with the two
networks set out in Figures 6.4 and 6.5, which have essentially the
same content, but with a rearrangement of terms.

The first modification deals with the fact that Figure 6.3 seems
to say that there are two kinds of sign (ARAL and SPECIAL),
and two independent kinds of answer (SURE BOUNDARY and SET
FORM), whereas in fact SURE BOUNDARY answers were just those
of ARAL sums and SET FORM answers those of   SPECIAL sums.
In the second modification the first and second levels of delicacy
have been transposed.   This produces quite radical changes in what
the network means.   The implications here are that Karen recognises
two distinct types of sums, and then categorises under these sub-
groups according to the SIGNS and ANSWERS.   As a result of
this transposition the number of paradigms is reduced to eighteen.
It is no longer possible to have Venn diagram answers to sums in
arithmetic.

Lastly, consider a third alternative, Figure 6.6, where the
network is more radically restructured in an attempt to better
delineate meanings.   Now the implication of this network is that
Karen differentiates SPECIAL and ARAL sums, and in addition recognises
division as a special case when the answer is located above the sum.
For all the other ARAL sums the answer is to be found either below or
at the end.   With this network the number of paradigms has been
further reduced to only thirteen.

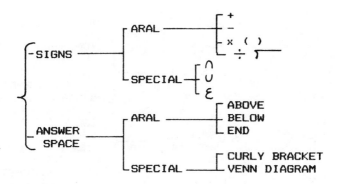

Figure 6.4   Modified version of Figure 6.3

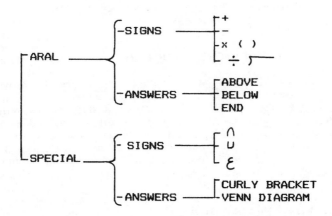

Figure 6.5   A second modified version
of Figure 6.3

        In attempting to represent Karen's views of sums, there is a real
choice to be made out of such alternatives, which differ not in what
the network terms are but in the distribution of the terms amongst
slightly changed structures of BARs and BRAs.   One can ask which
is the least bad view of Karen's view of sums.   Nancy Johnson would
argue that it is the first: that the network she proposed, and which
we have modified for illustrative purposes, does indeed sketch
something of Karen's cognitive scheme.

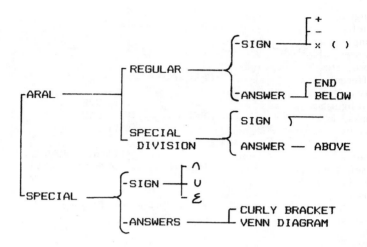

Figure 6.6   Third modified version of
              Figure 6.3

6.2 DATA AND NETWORK STRUCTURES

Data can be broken up into chunks of varying size, for example, a whole interview, parts of it or even single sentences from it.   In Section 6.2.1 the question of how a network analysis might manage such differences is discussed.   Data is also often patterned in various ways whether sequentially, causally or through some structure such as a hierarchy.   Possible representations of such patterns in network form are considered in Section 6.2.2 and 6.2.3 and problems of representation in Section 6.2.4.

6.2.1 Rank: Unit of Analysis

What is the unit of analysis in qualitative data?   In some cases this is hardly questionable, for the children's classifications of food items (Example 3.2) or children's comment about each other (Example 3.5).   At the opposite extreme if the data is a long text such as an interview transcript, as in the cases of the study of students' reactions (Example 3.1) or problem solving (Example 3.6) an important and very non-trivial part of the analysis is settling on the size, scope or boundaries of the elements of the data to be analysed.
        One will often find oneself naturally thinking of data as composed of parts; perhaps stories made up of episodes, themselves made up of events, with possible events built out of (say) persons and their interactions.   Such a pattern is sufficiently analogous to the linguistic concept of rank for it to be useful to borrow that term to refer to the distinction of size of unit in the formalised coding

language derived from a network. A definition of rank was given briefly in Chapter 2 section 2.4.4. However, by rank, linguists mean simply that paragraphs are made of sentences, which are made of clauses, which are made of word-groups, which are made of types of word, etc. The value of the idea is that at each size of unit, different kinds of meaning are relevant: it is at clause rank that passive distinguishes from active; at word rank that plural distinguishes from singular. Similarly, descriptions at different ranks, in our borrowed sense of the term, of qualitative data will usually be rather different in kind.

When carrying out an analysis it is important to be aware of whether the data is being looked at from within a rank, so looking at a set of features which describe the data all from the same level; or whether it is being considered from the point of view of being broken down into parts and sub-parts, so moving from one rank to another.

In example 3.1 about students' reactions to learning there are several shifts of rank. The students' stories are not analysed as a whole but are broken down into smaller sub-units of CLAUSE, with LINKS joining the clauses. However, even the CLAUSE was too large a unit for analysis and had to be broken down into smaller parts, a TOPIC and a COMMENT. Each time the unit of data to be analysed is broken into a smaller unit this can be seen as a shift of rank, a CLAUSE only being one part of the STORY and the TOPIC being a smaller chunk of the CLAUSE. The most obvious shift of rank in this network is the passage from strategy to descriptive networks. The former give a procedure for analysing the stories, whereas the latter describe the data itself.

For these same stories it is possible to imagine a very simple system at the rank of the whole story itself in that each was categorised as either a 'good' or 'bad' learning experience. To demonstrate the point, a further exploration at that rank might have looked somewhat like the network in Figure 6.7. This was not in fact done as it was decided that an analysis at this level would fail to capture necessary details and connections, making the analysis by some division into smaller parts a necessity.

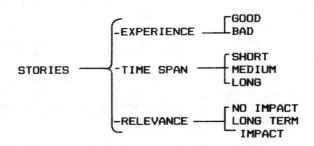

Figure 6.7 Distinctions within same rank

In Example 3.8, physics examination questions are described, with each description intended to apply to the whole question.   An alternative might in principle have been (and was indeed tried at an earlier stage in that work) to analyse any question firstly into steps: what situation the question put before one, what it gave as information, and what kind of solution process it required.   Thus a question might propose a typical experimental set-up, give data, and require recognition of a correct graph of the data.   Clearly, a network describing these components will differ markedly from one describing the question as a whole.

It is useful to develop the distinction between staying within one rank or shifting rank made in the previous two examples.   When a unit of data, whatever its size, is being described by features at the same rank these features will either refer to properties that are global, so describing the totality each time from different aspects; or will consider different kinds of the same totality.   So, for example, as in Figure 6.2 buildings can be described in terms of their usage, their size, or their location;   or, as in Figure 6.1, different types of buildings can be listed.   Thus a shift from left to right in a network is simply describing the thing that has gone before in a different manner, or saying that the same thing is now being described more delicately.

It is a different question when the unit of data being described is being broken down into smaller parts and so a shift in rank is being made.   If the example of buildings, used above, is analysed in this way one might say that a building is made up of a roof, doors and windows, giving the network in Figure 6.8.   In our terms, roof, doors and windows are at a rank below that of the whole building.   If the network now goes on, not to further divide these into their parts (doors into panels, locks, hinges, for example) but to distinguish kinds of roofs, doors and windows, we might have the network in Figure 6.9.

Notice that to use a BRA as in the two cases in Figures 6.8 and 6.9, to indicate parts rather than aspects, is to use it in a distinctive way, for which   the purist may prefer a new notation (a double bracket, perhaps).   This is an area of the notation which requires further work, both to see the usefulness of such a new type of bracket and to consider its implications at the level of formalism.

The linguists themselves do not have different notations to describe different ranks.   Halliday (1976) and other systemic linguists use networks to describe the typologies at each rank, but not the rank scale itself.   The description is then in the form of a collection of networks, at various ranks.

An interesting piece of work which involves the notion of rank is that of Sinclair and Coulthard (1975),   studying language in the classroom.   They make use of what is known as scale and category grammar (a precursor of systemic grammar), in their analysis.   For them the grammar of a lesson is somewhat analogous to that of a paragraph, being broken down into successively smaller chunks, such that at each size of chunk there are a range of types proper to that size of chunk.

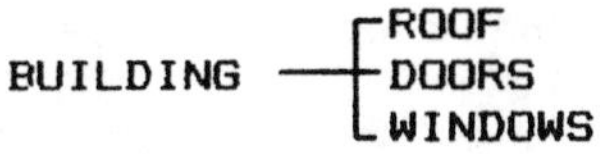

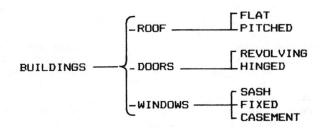

Figure 6.8   Shift of rank

Figure 6.9   Development of network
in Figure 6.8

Lessons, then, are analysed along a rank scale, which runs from transactions, of which the whole lesson is composed, down through exchanges, moves and finally the smallest unit of discourse, the act. Each rank above the lowest has a structure which can be expressed in terms of the units below.   Acts are units at the lowest rank of discourse corresponding to the grammatical unit, clause.   The three major classes of act (out of 21) are Elicitation, Informative and Directive, being the functional parallels of the grammatical clause categories interrogative, declarative and imperative.   Thus an Elicitation is an act that has the function of requesting a linguistic response, a Directive act is concerned with the control of action, that is, with requesting a non-linguistic response (close the door!) and an Informative act passes on information such as ideas, opinions, etc.

Moves are made of acts (at the rank below) and are themselves components of exchanges (at the rank above).   There are five classes of move which participate in two sorts of exchanges - Boundary and Teaching. Boundary exchanges are composed of Framing and Focus moves and Teaching exchanges consist of Opening, Answering and Follow-up moves.   We shall illustrate two of these moves by showing how they function in the classroom context.   A Framing move is made by a teacher indicating that he has finished one part of a lesson and is about to start the next.   Such a move is indicated by expressions such as "Right (silent pause)", or "Well (silent pause)".   When the teacher introduces children to what is going to happen he is making a Focus move, for example, "Today we are going to do two experiments". A Boundary exchange could consist of the Frame move given above, followed by the Focus.   Teaching, the other major class of exchange, can be defined as the individual stages by which the lesson progresses.   There are eleven classes of Teaching exchanges, six free and five bound, with bound exchanges differing from free in having no initiating move. Examples of free Teaching exchanges, made up of Opening, Answering and Follow-up moves, are "Teacher Inform" where the teacher is passing on various kinds of information to pupils; and "Checking" where the teacher tries to find out how children are getting on; whether they are listening, have finished their work, etc. "Teacher Elicit" and "Teacher Direct" are two other free exchanges. Of the five bound exchanges four are bound to "Teacher Elicit" and one to "Teacher Direct", free exchanges.

Finally, the next rank "Transaction" is composed of a Preliminary exchange, one or more Medial exchanges, and a Final exchange (the analysis here being, however, more tentative than that above). Lessons, composed of unordered and untypified transactions, are given no further analysis.

This brief summary shows that Sinclair and Coulthard succeed in constructing an analysis of classroom discourse which has a Chinese box (or Russian doll) structure, with each rank (or chunk) composed of elements inside it, of various types, themselves containing elements at the next lower rank, down to the lowest. Networks having this kind of formal structure are discussed in Chapter 7.

6.2.2 Describing Connections

Data comes in all sorts of patterns which are often revealed through the manner in which one chunk of data is linked to another. These connections can be of various kinds, for example, temporal, causal or conditional. Linguists have faced a problem of a similar kind in attempting to relate one element of a text to another. An example of such a linguistic analytic scheme is now developed in order to suggest resources which any analyst of qualitative data might find useful.

For a linguist, the way in which speech or writing hangs together is called cohesiveness. One obvious aspect of cohesion is the use of conjunctions: words such as 'and' 'then' and 'but', which join. More than one scheme for dealing with this has been proposed, an early one being Berry (1975). That outlined in Figure 6.10 is based upon a more extensive study by Halliday and Hasan (1976). Halliday and Hasan distinguish four main kinds of conjunction: ADDITIVE (and, also, or, that is, similarly, for instance ....), ADVERSATIVE (yet, though, but, however, rather, instead, anyhow .....), CAUSAL (so, then, hence, for, because .....) and TEMPORAL (then, next, after that, thereupon, soon, finally, ...) as shown in Figure 6.10.

It may be worth remarking that one important difference between this and other schemes is the promotion of ADVERSATIVE (i.e contrary to expectation) to a main category, possibly on the grounds that expectation plays a large role in shaping language in use. Expectation will often be important in many social or psychological contexts, and such an emphasis seems generally worth consideration. Other features may be less generally applicable, and one could argue that PURPOSE, while acceptable under CAUSAL for the analysis of linguistic cohesion, might deserve a larger place of its own in other analyses. But it is only by seeing such a scheme laid out that such ideas can easily be provoked.

It is not suggested that this or any other scheme is necessarily the best. It will often be convenient to develop ad-hoc schemes of links, as suggested by commonsense and by the way the material to be described is conceptualised. Thus work on teachers' expectations will naturally suggest an expectation type of link and good sense will supply links such as coincidence and accident.

In looking at students' reactions to their experiences in learning physics (Example 3.1), clauses representing parts of stories were joined with linking terms representing cause, time, parallelism. Such links were needed because having broken the stories into bits - clauses, some formal way was required to represent how they went together. The terms used are clearly related to, but do not use all of, the kind of linguistic scheme shown in Figure 6.10.

It could be that the work done on both problem solving in chemistry (Example 3.6) and children's alternative frameworks for force and energy (Example 3.7) would have taken a rather different turn if some form of linkage had been used. In the chemistry problem solving case causal and temporal links are immediately suggested by the nature of the work itself. Mike Watts' development of networks for force and energy might have incorporated links that were causal,

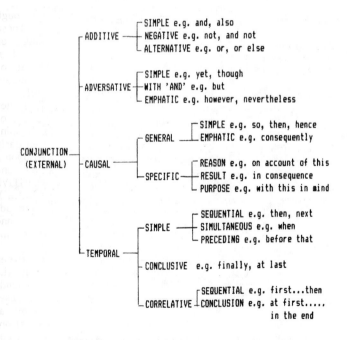

Figure 6.10   Network for conjunction

additive and adversative.   These remarks are of course purely speculative.

Connections or links of the kind just discussed can be used to join together coded descriptions to make a whole in cases where the data is best regarded as made of linked parts (see Section 2.2.1). Thus the linguistic network of Figure 6.10 might be used to generate code of the form:

> BECAUSE some event
> AFTER some event
> THEN some event

in which codes for parts of the data are strung in a sequence with conjunctions.   If the time sequence is all that matters, then a simple recursive network describing the data may do, such that a whole sequence is coded in the form:

> some event
> some event
> some event

with the order, usually a time order, left implicit in the stringing together of descriptions.

It may be useful to arrange for the network to do the equivalent of numbering items in a sequence.   Thus the code:

> 1 some event
> 2 some event
> 3 some event

could be generated by a network of the type shown in Figure 6.11. One might say that the TIME part of this network functions as a kind of clock.   Naturally one can use any suitable terms to mark time or sequence, such as those shown in Figure 6.12.

The example in Figure 6.12 is a reminder that sequence itself can have an inner structure (here, trivially, WEEKDAY vs WEEKEND). Such clocks, if they do no more than make explicit what is left implicit in the ordering of items in code in a sequence, are at most a minor convenience.   However, if later analysis will be concerned with patterns in time, they may be essential, for example, if one will want

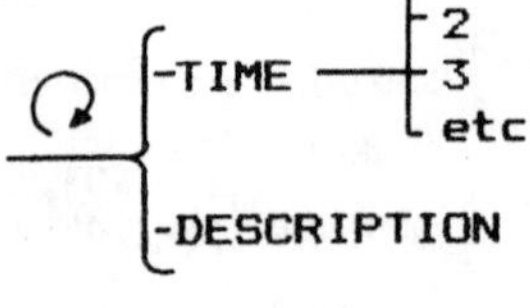

Figure 6.11   Network using simple
                 time regulator

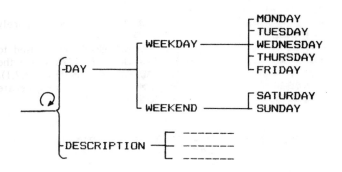

Figure 6.12   Network using another
time regulator

to know how often various types of thing happened (say) second, or on Tuesdays, or at weekends.   The example of problem solving in chemistry (Example 3.6) is a clear possible case in point (e.g. does evaluation happen much before the end of a problem?).

Such clocks may be even less trivial if the data needs representations of more than one kind of link at the same time.   Thus a study of school organisation and policy making could well need both cause and effect and time markers so that codes say something like:

(2) PRESENT (AUTUMN 82)
        SITUATION   CHANGES IN SCHOOL ORGANISATION
(3) PRESENT (AUTUMN 82)
        WHEN NEW SCHOOL POLICY DRAWN UP
(1) PAST   (SUMMER 82)
        BECAUSE APPOINTMENT OF NEW HEAD
(4) FUTURE   (JANUARY 83)
        ANTICIPATING LEA EXPENDITURE CUTS

in which causes look forwards and backwards in time so that a natural sequence of codes is not in a simple time order.   If the events were simply classified in the order of happening, they would follow the numbers given in brackets.   The examples given here are mainly notional, since such matters have not been a particularly serious issue for any of the studies set out in Chapter 3, but it nevertheless seems worth pointing out some of the devices a network analyst could exploit, if only to suggest ideas.

6.2.3   Terms with Explicit or Implicit Ordering

A network may be required to express ordered relations between terms within it.   Both the networks in Figure 6.13 contain terms which for those who understand them have an implicit order.

159

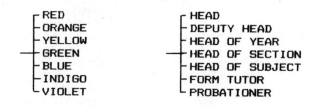

Figure 6.13   **Networks with implicit ordering**

One may wish, however, for the network to express something of the nature of the ordering. The network in Figure 6.14 attempts to describe the hierarchy by making a distinction between area and level of responsibility.

In Figure 6.14 the area of responsibility has been separated off from the level of responsibility. The hierarchical aspect rests with the level of responsibility, but the implication now is that area of responsibility has the full range of levels independently of the others.

A different approach would be simply to number positions in a hierarchy, and then describe kinds of involvement and areas of concern. A person may have different involvements in different areas, so the activity systems are made recursive. Thus having assigned someone a position in the hierarchy the details of various activities are filled in by recursion through each area. A headmaster would now appear, not as HEAD, but as a person in the first place in the hierarchy, with ultimate responsibility for every area of activity. The probationary teacher would be located towards the bottom of the hierarchy, a functionary in respect of teaching and pastoral care whilst probably uninvolved in both curriculum development and extra school liaison.

A characteristic of such a use of networks is that almost everything of interest will now be found in the codes. The network

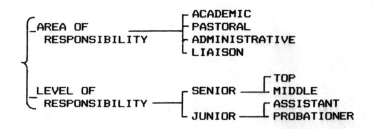

Figure 6.14   **Problems of network description of hierarchy**

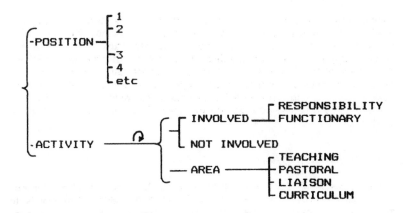

Figure 6.15   Alternative version of
              Figure 6.14

does not say, for example, what a Head of Department does;   indeed it
says that anyone can do anything.

In Example 6.5, had Martin Monk had data on power hierarchies
within cliques of pupils, he might well have required some such
solution.

6.2.4 Changes in Structure in Time

Section 6.2.2 discussed networks with time sequence and 6.2.3 networks
involving hierarchical structure.   A problem related to both, though
distantly is that of using networks to represent changing structures
in time.   One solution appears in Example 6.9 in which Halliday
studies developing grammars of a child's language, each a structure in
its own right, representing them by a series of networks one for each.
Piagetian data would be another example of the same kind of
problem.   It may be that the solution of a series of changing
networks is a good one, but it has to be admitted that the networks
themselves do not represent the process or mechanism of change,
showing it only by becoming different.   To do more, of course, would
require an analysis of the process of change, to produce which would
in many cases be to make a major contribution to theory.   We have no
such example to offer, but the possibility may be worth consideration.

6.3 CODING AND COUNTING

In most of what has been discussed in this chapter the network is
viewed as a result in its own right, with the categories and how they
are structured being the focus.   It is sometimes useful and

interesting, however, to view a network as a tool for further analysis. Networks generate codes and it is possible that the patterns of the codes have an interesting structure which in itself might suggest ideas for further development of the network, as discussed in Section 6.3.1. Further analysis can also look at how frequently certain patterns or paradigms occur and possible relations between them, and Section 6.3.2 describes this possibility. Finally, Section 6.3.3 discusses the nature of code: what code says and what it says it about.

6.3.1 Patterns in Codes

In the example in Section 6.2.1 Sinclair and Coulthard propose precise classes of elements which are the constituents of elements at the rank above, but leave open how often such classes are used. Thus one teacher might use many Teaching exchanges, or only one or two, between Boundary exchanges. He might often follow an Informative act by an Eliciting act, or the reverse. One might call such patterns, if found, part of a teaching style.

A network will often take a weaker position than a scale and category analysis about the patterning of items. At some level, the network presents only possible choices of term, and not the way they are in fact chosen. It may insist (with a BRA) on the presence of certain types, or it may not. Thus, after a network has been constructed, there may be further work worth doing on the patterns found in the actual choices made from it.

An example may make the point clearer, and we shall consider possible developments in Example 3.6, that of problem solving in chemistry. Although one output might be counts of occurrences of particular terms, there are other alternatives that look to information other than single counts.

It is possible that by closer examination of codes of the students' protocols, patterns to do with the nature of problem solving can be observed. These patterns would then be independent of patterning that might be present in the network itself. A (hypothetical) example would be looking for patterns of evaluation: when and how do students make evaluative moves? One might find that evaluation occurred systematically or it might be much more sporadic. It might very often occur after the student had tried a certain calculation - as a sort of check. It might show different patterning in well-structured problems and in open-ended problems, and so on. Another example might be to look at how data is used: at whether data provided in the question is used or ignored, or at how other data based on the original data is incorporated into the problem solution. A third possibility would be to look at where, when and how often new information is introduced.

It is also possible that looking at the patterns in coded data would suggest ideas for restructuring the network. The patterns might suggest important new distinctions that had not been obvious until the data itself had been organised by being coded.

6.3.2 Ways of Counting

Given a single item of data to be coded on a non-recursive network, we just code a single paradigm.   When many items are coded, counting of features is possible, as it is also for single items if the network is recursive.   There may be a need to test statistical models of counts.

The simplest way of counting is to just let the coded items be counted at the terminals, but this sort of counting loses the distinctions and co-selections that the network allows.   In order to be able to count and still retain those distinctions it may be better to take counts of paradigms.   An example of the difference is shown in Figure 6.16.

By virtue of the fact that networks have several levels of delicacy worked into their construction and that at each successive layer the categories tend to proliferate, the level of delicacy at which one counts can be reduced so as to reduce the number of categories and to increase the number counts in any category.   The process is essentially that of collapsing a contingency table.   An advantage of doing this guided by the levels of delicacy represented in a network is that the process is more visible and so easier to reflect on.   One can decide both which categories should be merged, and at what stage they should be merged.

The two examples in Chapter 3 that have actually made counting a definite goal in their work are those of Janet Holland and Martin Monk.   In Janet Holland's case with her work on children's

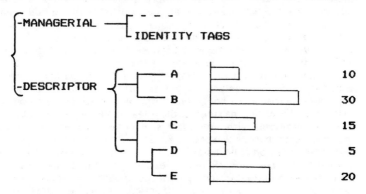

(a) counts of terminals

AC	AD	AE	BC	BD	BE
5	1	4	10	4	16

(a) counts of paradigms

Figure 6.16   Ways of counting

classification strategies for food stuffs, she counts both at the terminals and, through implication with the distinctions of CONTEXT DEPENDENT and CONTEXT INDEPENDENT, at the first level of delicacy. The counts that are made in Martin Monk's example on peer reported comments are made at each and every successive level of delicacy and, unlike Janet Holland in her work, he chooses to test for statistical significance drawing up the dimensions of his contingency tables according to the terms in the managerial part of his network that gives identification tags to the children. Neither of these examples uses what we have chosen to call counts of paradigms.

6.3.3 What Does a Code Say?

Networks generate codes, and an analyst ends up coding data. These two processes are quite different, the first purely formal and arbitrary, the second the essence of analysis using networks. But codes are not simply the data in another form: if they were, the networks would be irrelevant. It is important, then to be clear about the status of codes. Consider an analyst starting with a very long transcript of an interview or pages of a student's script, and triumphantly finishing the day with a single page full of codes 'representing' the original data, looking much more manageable than the original. One problem with such codes is that once they are there on the page it is easy to forget what they represent, and to fall into the trap of thinking that the relation between code and data is much simpler and more direct than it really is. It seems as if the data has somehow been directly translated into code.

Compare the relations of network to code, and of data to code. To pass from a network paradigm to the code is simple: one follows the realisation rules which simply state how the paradigm should be encoded. Such rules are completely arbitrary and are chosen solely for convenience. Although one form of realisation rule could be to write out the entire paradigm, the idea of having a code to replace lengthy paradigms with something shorter or more expressive is often valuable (see Chapter 2, Section 2.4.2).

The relation of paradigm to data is much more problematic. The crucial test for a network is to see that each and every paradigm can be instanced and whether or not absence of instances makes any sort of sense as discussed in Chapter 4 (Section 4.6) and Chapter 8 (Section 8.2.1). The analyst needs to build sets of criteria for what counts as instances. Achieving this is long and difficult, not because the terms of a paradigm are unclear but because the data itself does not always match a waiting slot.

The matching problem can be illustrated from Example 3.1 that concerns students' reactions to learning. One paradigm describes students' feelings having to do with inner success. Statements by two students, one saying, "I felt as though I was getting on top of it, as though I had got somewhere", and another, "I felt as though I had achieved something even though it was a very little", were both counted as instances of this paradigm as were many others like them.

Criteria for this category were that the student expressed some feeling related to a personal sense of success, not tied to feelings of success as recognised by others. Despite differences between the two expressions of feelings above, the paradigm of 'inner success' was meant to capture something important they have in common.

When such a match has been established between data and paradigm, only then can the appropriate code be given to that piece of data. Codes are thus a long way from the data, even though in some sense they 'stand for' it. They derive from the analyst's view of data, not from the data, and this view will usually be more general and abstract than the data and will also need, in order to be useful, to have lost some of the data's richness and complexity.

When codes are chosen to be expressive or words taken from data are used, confusion about their status is even easier to fall into, despite their advantage of being easier to remember. Thus, a network dealing with school achievement might have a paradigm to describe children completing 5 years of secondary schooling without getting any qualifications at all. 'Underachievers' as a code for this paradigm would seem, at first sight, to express it well. It is, however, a word which has considerable force, and means rather different things to different people. Care would need to be taken that the definition of the paradigm is not lost by conferring the meaning from some other usage onto the code. More specifically dangers can arise when - because of its expressive power or use of words from data - the code conveys what may seem to be criteria for a direct match of code to data, neglecting criteria for data instancing the paradigm that the code expresses. In this way 'underachievers' could become children who only get grade B at A-level, or who do not get grade 1 at O-level, and so on.

It is crucial to constantly be aware that codes are no more than a convenient way of expressing paradigms. Generating codes from the network is a straightforward process, bound by rules. Giving a code to data is the final step in a lengthy, critical process of creating paradigms that can be instantiated in the data, a process governed not by rules but by the analyst's ideas, judgments and perceptions.

Chapter 7

VARIETIES OF REPRESENTATION

Apart from the introduction of the network formalism in Chapter 2, we have otherwise done little to situate analysis using networks in relation to other approaches, to other formalisms, or to other disciplines. Whilst this balance reflects the main orientation and aim of the book, it is worthwhile to stand back and take a more abstract view of the general nature of networks, and it is this which the present chapter attempts.

The account cannot be exhaustive, nor can it go very deep, since it turns out that to provide it one has to trespass in a number of very different, seemingly unrelated fields including logic, mathematics, computer science and linguistics, not to mention psychology and sociology. We can claim no special expertise in most of them, but have nevertheless, however incautiously, attempted to extract a few general lessons from our understanding of them.

7.1 TWO METAPHORS

To use a network at all is to hold that one can and should produce a representation of a complex structure, and what the various fields mentioned above have in common are some similarities in the way they conceive the nature of complexity. These similarities, as we see them, function not at the level of shared factual assumptions, but rather at the level of certain common guiding metaphors, amongst which we identify two in particular, the 'grammatical' and the 'computational' metaphors discussed below. Later parts of the chapter will show how, by following these metaphors through, one can identify formal parallels between networks and formalisms developed for other purposes, and can also sharpen a little the vague sense that networks are 'something like' other ways of doing things.

7.1.1 The Grammatical Metaphor

Deriving in large part from Wittgenstein, the metaphor of a 'grammar' for those deep structural features of situations which give them meaning and coherence has made its presence felt in a variety of disciplines, and can perhaps be seen implicitly at work in others. Thus it is common to find philosophers writing of the 'grammar' of a concept; it is no accident that one collection of anthropological essays is entitled 'Rules and Meanings' (Douglas 1973), nor that writing about language and the social context shares many of the same assumptions about what is worth investigating (for example Giglioli 1972).

Probably the force of the metaphor lies in the way actual grammar - the rules of a language - is just what makes meaning possible at all, is the common property of a whole community, is itself an extended and complex structure, and, whilst 'well known' to every native speaker, is in large part sub-conscious. So 'grammar' lends itself well as a metaphor for strong but hidden rules which structure or mediate meaningful acts. Just such a notion underlies several structural approaches to sociology, for example Network Analysis (with the term 'Network' used in another sense from ours). See for example Marsden and Lin (1982) or Knoke and Kuklinski (1982). The network notation we use derives of course from a grammatical notation.

In reverse, some linguists have felt that their work has something to say about psychology or sociology. Thus Chomsky's analysis of deep, structural and abstract properties of any grammar suggest to him implications for the nature of mind (Chomsky 1972), whilst by contrast Halliday's account of the nature of language is at the same time an account of social meanings (Halliday 1978). Here of course, the role of grammar is actual, not metaphorical.

The grammatical metaphor clearly pervades the methodology suggested in the present book. In an important sense, a network is precisely a contrived grammar for an artificial language to describe data. Metaphorically, one might conceive of some networks as themselves a kind of 'grammar' of the situation described; as laying out some of its deep structural organisation. The examples in Chapter 3 are more modest than this in their claims, but several nevertheless share some notion of getting a network to express at least something significant about structure.

7.1.2 The Computational Metaphor

In the present century, much of the new thinking about how to handle, represent and organise complexity has been informed by a computational metaphor, with structures, strategies and formalisms derving from computation being used in models for thought, language, memory and even personality.

Computational thinking has also greatly influenced mathematical logic, which in its origins was itself seen as expressing 'laws of thought'. Psychology and logic have always had a special relationship (strong in Piaget, but present elsewhere) and the relationship has strengthened rather than weakened in the last few decades. Mathematical logic, now embracing the logic of computing machines, has grown extensive and has been applied in many ways. An early example from the 1940's is McCulloch and Pitts' use of the logic of switching elements to model neural structures (see Minsky 1972 or McCulloch 1965). More recently, computational models have come to form the essential basis of a whole way of doing psychology (first called Information-Processing, now Cognitive Science - see for example Wason and Johnson-Laird 1977), and computer programs that (in some sense) comprehend natural language, solve problems, discover patterns or make plausible inferences have been developed (see for instance Minsky 1968 for early work, Boden 1977 for a broad review, and Michie 1979 for examples of recent work).

There are those who find the computational metaphor distasteful, dangerous or irrelevant (perhaps all three). One need not be in sympathy with it, however, to accept that its use has enlarged and better defined our notion of complexity: that a good place to seek ideas about complex representations of complex data is computing.

The two metaphors are also rather intimately related. It was mathematical logic that inspired Chomsky's linguistic work, and reciprocally work in linguistics (e.g. Fillmore 1968) has been exploited by those attempting to write computer programs with realistic language capabilities (Winograd 1972, Schank and Colby 1973, Findler 1970).

7.1.3 Relationship to Networks

The rest of the chapter discusses various aspects of the relationship of networks to the other areas mentioned. In 7.2 the nature of the connection of networks with linguistics is examined from a general point of view. In 7.3, turning aside briefly, some remarks are offered about a comparison with one seemingly related psychological theory. 7.4 returns to the main theme, now in more detail, looking at formalisms from mathematics, logic and linguistics, and showing how the network notation can be translated into other forms. It is shown that the network notation agrees well with widely used fundamental logical structures, and that a beginning can be made on characterising the 'power' of a network in a formal way. Finally 7.5 broadens the issues again, looking at how networks compare with some other attempts to represent structures of complex relationships.

7.2 NETWORKS AND LINGUISTICS

Whilst acknowledging the debt to linguistics, we have warned elsewhere in the book of the dangers of seeing the connection too literally. This section discusses the general nature of the relation of our use of networks to linguistics.

To most people, perhaps, 'linguistics' suggests the minute study of the origins of words or of rare dialects, and 'grammar' is strongly associated with rules, often pedantic, of correct usage. To the modern linguist, both are grave misconceptions.

Grammar, to the linguist, is descriptive, not normative: it

describes the rules a language community actually uses, rather than telling such a community what its usage ought to be.   Though other people may have preferences for or objections to certain forms, the linguist's job is to study those forms.   He will not regard some form used for communication and understood by others as breaking a rule, but rather as obeying a different rule, which it may be his business to make explicit.   Such an attitude does not differ from that of almost any researcher towards his or her subject matter.

The term 'rule' is here being used in the sense, then, not of something it is wrong-headed or ignorant to disobey, but of a structural principle of a language.   Indeed, at least since de Saussure (widely regarded as the founder of modern linguistics), linguists have primarily attended to structures in language: to the way language is patterned and organised, and to how languages exploit such patterns each in their own ways.

The achievement of Chomsky was to show that, granted sufficient idealisation, natural languages could be analysed as formal systems akin to the formal systems of mathematics.   Our networks betray some of this influence, in regarding a network as a formal specification of a data-description language.   The connection operates at the formal level too, in that the network formalism can be translated into that of Chomsky (see section 7.4).   Chomsky, however, has been primarily concerned with the analysis of syntax;   with the sequential ordering of language structures, whereas our concern in the analysis of qualitative data has been with the choice of terms and structures for the description of data.   For this reason, amongst linguists we have found most help in the ideas of a different school - the systemic linguists - whose interests have focussed mainly on meaning as a social interaction, deriving from de Saussure and from Firth the central notion of meaning as choice in context (see 2.5).   Their network notation expresses just this principle, which is why we have found it and much of their terminology convenient.

It needs stressing once more what, despite the linguistic influence, the analysis of data using networks is not.   It is not an analysis of the language of data.   It is not concerned in any fundamental way with data as language-data.   It is not specially oriented to research problems, for example classroom interaction, in which language plays an important role.   Naturally, most qualitative data is something said or written, but for our purposes the data is what someone meant, not the words or forms used to convey that meaning.   It may not be clear what was meant, but then the solution would be to ask for clarification, not to study the text more minutely.

This is not to say that an analysis using networks cannot have a linguistic turn, but only to say that there is no essential need for it to have one.   Indeed, example 3.9 in Chapter 3 outlines two linguistically oriented studies, and in example 3.2 Janet Holland mentions her debt to Bernstein's sociolinguistic theory.

It has to be said that many linguists would reject the views of the systemic school as any kind of adequate account of language.   The main force of such criticism centres on whether the terms in networks describing grammar point to anything really there in language, or whether they are little more than glosses on what seems to be going on. We shall not take sides in any such debate, since its substance does not concern or affect uses of networks for non-linguistic purposes. Its form, however, is of importance, since whatever the domain of an analysis, the question of whether the descriptive terms used represent real or fancied distinctions cannot be avoided. Chapter 8 takes up such issues at some length.

7.3 REPERTORY GRIDS AND CONSTRUCTS

One psychological theory in which one might see the 'grammatical metaphor' at work (7.1) is Kelly's personal construct theory (e.g. Kelly 1955). Certainly the theory holds that a person's ideas - indeed his self - are a complex interrelated structure, and proposes ways of investigating and representing that structure. Interest centres on the structure as such, on how and why things relate, not merely in elaborating more and more complex detail. The theory holds that the structure is rational, held together by intelligible rules or principles, so that to study a person in this way is to study the 'grammar' of his unique rationality.

Not surprisingly, then, we have been asked whether there is some connection or relation between the analysis of qualitative data using networks, and the use of personal construct theory's main tool, namely repertory grids. This section sets out the similarities and differences, as we see them.

There is no sense in setting up a competition between networks and repertory grids, in our view. Firstly, personal construct theory is a whole psychological theory, to be judged in its own right, whereas networks are a technique, not a theory. Within construct theory, the theoretical entities called 'constructs' are bipolar contrasts a person makes in dividing up the world in a - for him - meaningful way. Repertory grids are a collection of methods of eliciting and then encoding such contrasts for further study or reflection. The essential bipolarity of constructs arises from the theory, and the repertory technique is designed accordingly.

Briefly, when using a repertory grid (see e.g. Fransella and Bannister 1977) a number of elements relevant to the subject of the enquiry are put before the respondent, who is invited to reveal a construct by explaining how - for him - there is a way in which two (or more) elements are alike and are thereby different from a third (or more). Then all (or some) elements are marked as belonging to one side or pole of the construct or to the other. The same set of elements can be construed in many ways, and the repertory grid encodes which elements partipate in which way in the various constructs.

In a further stage of analysis, structure may be sought in the grid, looking for similarities or differences between constructs, as shown by the ways the chosen elements fall amongst them. Naturally, constructs themselves, previously elicited, can be used as elements so as to seek constructs of constructs, getting at structure in that way, rather than or in addition to pattern-seeking analysis of a grid.

One difference is that we have not proposed networks as a scheme for eliciting data at all, but rather as a post-hoc framework for analysis. This is not to say that networks could not be exploited in such a way, whether to express the structure of a questionnaire, or as some kind of tool to guide questions and notate answers, but we have no experience of doing so.

Of course, one can use a repertory grid technique without subscribing to personal construct theory. In that case, one ought to have some reason for holding that relevant constructs are usefully regarded as bipolar. Further (and for those who do subscribe to the theory) if structure is sought by mathematical analysis of the grid, it needs to be recognised that different mathematical methods will extract different kinds of structure, so that one needs again some reason for selecting a method.

An underlying similarity between the idea of construct and the network notation is clearly the notion of meaning in contrast. A construct emphasises a single difference, however, whereas the BAR notation, and the idea of a system, allows a number of different but related distinctions, each dependent on the presence of the others, to be expressed. Of course constructs may be involved in relations more complex than a bipolar distinction, but this has to show up as relations between individually bipolar relations. There is also perhaps (though this is less clear) some parallel between the notion of delicacy and the locating of constructs of constructs. That is, some 'low-level' constructs might be found to be elements in 'higher level' constructs in something like the way systems at the more delicate levels can belong to less delicate systems.

Taking now the BRA notation, there is probably more difference than similarity if one asks what it and the idea of simultaneity would look like in relation to constructs. Certainly a person has many constructs, but the idea in construct theory is to go from there to further construct-like relations between them, not to arrive (as with a BRA) at relatively independent dimensions. The difference has most to do, it seems to us, with the difference in intent: in work with constructs to find out what people think and with networks to clarify and set down what one wants oneself to say.

In summary, it seems to us that not too much should be made either of the similarities or of the differences. It is right to accept a common concern with meanings as personal, and with the virtues of attempting to make them explicit. It would be wrong to draw any very strong comparison between, say, a Kellyian psychologist trying to find out, and help an anxious patient to see, how he perceives friends and relations, and an educational researcher trying to find useful and meaningful ways to describe data about, say classroom management, by building a network. One deep connection (shared not only with personal construct theory) is that just as construct theory insists on constructs being proper to the individual - as his way of understanding the world - so we, in the same spirit, have repeatedly insisted on any analysis being regarded as proper to the analyst - once again, as his way of understanding the world.

171

7.4 SOME FORMALISM

We now turn to a brief sketch of the relationship of networks to two fundamental mathematical formalisms, graph theory and production systems, both of which have found applications of the kind previously mentioned (7.1.2).

There is no escaping the fact that mathematics charms some by its elegance, power and clarity but repels others who see in it only incomprehensible and meaningless play with symbols. Nor is there space here to give (even if we were able to) such explanations from first principles as might help the second group. Thus this section is restricted to mentioning the main points of contact, and to stating a few elementary results.

7.4.1 Graphs and Categories

A systemic network belongs to a well known general mathematical species: that called graphs. Formally, a graph is any collection of lines joining a set of nodes - a railway map is a clear case in point. In a network, the lines have a sense of direction (from one term to the next) so that a network is a directed graph.

To avoid confusion we should mention in passing that in graph theory the term 'network' has a special use, meaning a graph whose lines are associated with some numerical quantity, such as the rate of flow of fluid in interconnected pipes. We are not using the term 'network' in this sense at all.

What kind of structure a graph represents depends on the interpretation given to its nodes and lines. One simple interpretation could be that of a 'walk' through the graph, going from node to node by choosing just one of the lines leaving the node one is currently at. Such an interpretation immediately allows a network composed only of BARs to be represented (almost trivially) as a directed tree graph as in Figure 7.1.

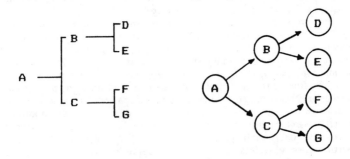

Figure 7.1   Directed tree graph of a
network composed of BARS

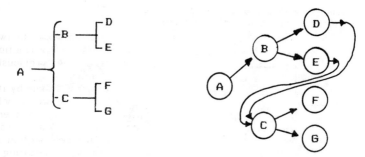

Figure 7.2   One way of representing a
network containing a BRA

To deal with a network containing BRAs is less trivial. Figure
7.2 shows one inelegant device, shortly to be rejected, for doing so.
Keeping the previous interpretation, entry to the second term C on the
BRA is forced, as it must be from the meaning of the BRA notation, by
having extra lines from all the places (D and E) one can reach from
the first term B, back to C. (There being only one exit line from D or
E there is no alternative exit from either.)
    The graph in Figure 7.2 has an asymmetry which is a poor
representation of a BRA. The same difficulty has led graph theorists
to ask whether an alternative interpretation would be preferable,
leading to a simpler graph. Happily for the network notation, the
relevant alternative is to introduce three types of node which happen
to correspond precisely to the meanings given to a BAR, a BRA and a
terminal. That is, the three types allowed are:

(i)   nodes containing just a terminal
(ii) nodes from which one must exit along just one of
         the outgoing lines
(iii) nodes from which one must exit along all the
         outgoing lines.

    Figure 7.3 illustrates the close correspondence there now is
between a network and its graph drawn using these three types of node.
    This extension to three types of node is related to a development
of graph theory known as category theory, which as its name suggests
studies the abstract form of the act of naming or labelling.   The
theory recognises again just three fundamental types of category:

(i)   single elements   e.g. D, E, F, G
(ii) unions of categories   e.g. B = D, E
(iii) products of categories   e.g. A = BC

These fundamental types of category correspond to the three types of
node mentioned, and thus also to terminals, BARs and BRAs.   Thus

the main network notation is in accord with the basic formalism of a relevant mathematical structure.

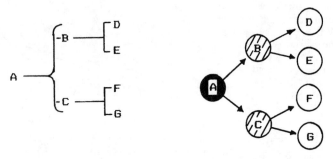

Figure 7.3   Graph using three types
of node (compare 7.2)

The computer programme BARBARA (Grize 1981) in fact stores a network as a graph, using the three types of node as in Figure 7.3.   Indeed, such graphs defining allowed combinations of symbols are widely used in the whole class of computer programmes called compilers, one of whose jobs it is to check expressions typed in by a programmer for correctness in terms of the computer language (e.g. PASCAL) being used.

Note finally that graph theory also allows recursion, in that a line can point back to a node 'earlier' in the graph, through which one has previously passed to reach the backward-pointing line.   Thus a recursive graph contains a closed circuit.

Graph and category theory have many applications, and some of their uses in building complex representational structures are discussed further in section 7.5.

7.4.2 Production Systems

What has turned out to be one of the most influential suggestions in logical formalism was made by Emil Post in 1943 (see Minsky 1972 for an extended account).   The idea was to regard the symbols of a formal expression as generated by a set of replacement rules, called productions.   It can well be illustrated by one of its best known applications, a primitive Chomsky-like grammar:

S ⟶	NP	VP	N ⟶	boy	
			N ⟶	girl	
VP ⟶	V	NP	V ⟶	likes	
			V ⟶	hates	
NP ⟶	D	N	D ⟶	that	
			D ⟶	this	

Given the start S, the first rule allows replacing it by one NP (noun phrase) followed by one VP (verb phrase). The VP can then be replaced by a V (verb) followed by an NP, and the NP by a D (determiner) and a N (noun), giving D N V NP, which then becomes D N V D N by replacing the second NP. Replacing the symbols D, N, V by one each of their possibilities, we get sentences such as:

> this boy likes that girl
> that girl hates that boy
> this boy likes this boy   etc.

Francois Grize has shown (Grize 1981) that the network notation can be translated into the notation of production systems. Figure 7.4 shows the elementary cases and their translations: more complex cases can be translated by forming suitable combinations. The translation only works, obviously, if terms in the network appear finally as items in the strings produced. Thus such a translation does not apply to the networks of systemic linguists, who adjoin to a network a set of

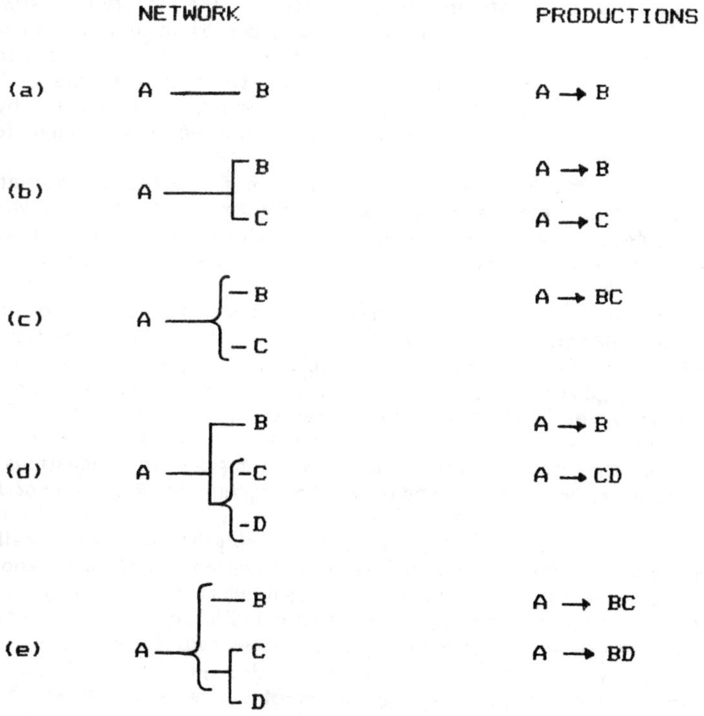

NETWORK   **PRODUCTIONS**

(a)   A ——— B   A → B

(b)   A ⌐ B   A → B
            L C   A → C

(c)   A { ─ B   A → BC
            ─ C

(d)   A ┤ ─ B   A → B
            ├ ─ C   A → CD
            └ ─ D

(e)   A { ─ B   A → BC
            ├ C   A → BD
            └ D

Figure 7.4   Elementary networks and their
              translations as productions

'realisation rules' which transform selection of a term into a surface item or structure in speech or writing in a more complex way. The present analysis is restricted to networks in which the realisation rules have the trivial form "copy the terms selected into the code". It may be noted that the translations illustrate the way BARs and BRAs form, respectively, union and product categories (Section 7.4.1).

Chomsky pointed out that, if the grammar of a language is defined by a set of productions, one can define types of language by placing restrictions on allowed kinds of productions. The stronger the restrictions, the weaker is the corresponding language type. A much used hierarchy of languages (Chomsky 1956) in which each type is a member of any type listed above it but not vice-versa, is:-

Type 0	No restrictions	
Type 1	Context-dependent grammars: No production effects contraction, i.e. absence of symbols never expresses the presence of a feature.	
Type 2	Phrase-structure or context-free grammars: Above restrictions; in addition the string on the left of a production can only be non-terminal.	
Type 3	Regular grammars: Above restrictions; in addition the string on the left must be non-terminal, and the string on the right must be either a terminal, or a terminal followed by a non-terminal.	

By terminal strings are meant those which appear in the final 'sentences' of the language, after eliminating non-terminals by successive applications of productions in which the latter appear on the left. The two types correspond to terminal and non-terminal terms of a network.

It follows at once that a network composed of BARs and BRAs (so that selection of a terminal is never conditional on selection of another) must define a language of type 2, or a context-free grammar. Such a language is 'context-free' in the sense that the grammar allowing some final expression is never conditional on that final expression. It is known that English is not context-free in this sense, but that (for example) PASCAL is. Chomsky hypothesises that a central part, but not the whole, of the grammar of any language is context-free.

Those with mathematical inclinations may be diverted by asking what networks which define regular grammars must look like. Figure 7.5 shows the form of the answer: the network must be built out of elements containing no more than is shown in Figure 7.5, each element joined to another like it from a place like N1 to a place like S.

Clearly, many simpler networks are also regular. A single BAR is perhaps the simplest, the grammar of a 'language' in which all sentences have only one word and no structure. The essence of a regular grammar is that (as Figure 7.5 shows) every move along the network either gives such a one-term label (i.e. A1, or A2 etc.) or it gives another one-term label (B1 or B2 etc.) plus further labels

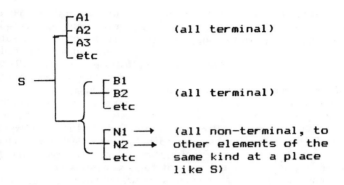

Figure 7.5   Allowed general form of an element
              of a network defining a regular
              (type 3) grammar

(following N1, N2 etc.) of the kind here described.   In effect a
regular grammar has layers of strata at each of which one assigns a
simple single-term description and passes to the next stratum.   Such a
language allows one to give a simple description at some level, and
then to proceed to another level and do the same again.

It would appear to be plausible that some kinds of hierarchical
structures (Bloom's taxonomy might be an example - Bloom et al 1956)
might be representable as regular grammars, in that one can envisage
such a network giving either a simple low level description to an
item, or a low level description plus a higher level one, and so on.

We may conclude this diversion by noting that recursion is also
allowed in a network defining a regular grammar, illustrating the
point by a classic mathematical example shown in Figure 7.6 (the
network is ours;   the productions are well-known).

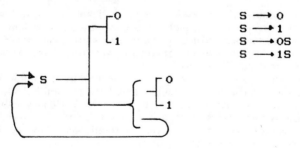

Figure 7.6   Network and productions
              for binary numbers

It is not hard to see that the network or productions generate the binary numbers. The simplest output is O or 1; the next is O or 1 followed by O or 1; and so on, giving amongst others

0   1   10   11   100   101   110   111   etc.

(The network does not exclude trivial identities, such as producing 001, 01 and 1).

We conclude that a network exploiting only BARs and BRAs and the simple realisation rule mentioned before, will define a context-free or type 2 language of description. Allowing recursion the converse is true though this has not been demonstrated here. The restrictions of regularity produce a naturally stratified structure. Should network terminals be used in input conditions, the language is no longer context-free. There appears to be scope for further study of these formal matters, which although not appropriate here, might usefully attempt to define suitable levels of complexity of network form.

Production systems have interest beyond such formal and linguistic concerns. They have been used as the basis of automatic theorem provers and of the computer language PROLOG now finding educational applications, as the form for the knowledge base of computer systems designed to have 'expert' knowledge, and as models for the structure of human cognition (for examples see Michie 1979, Newell and Simon 1972). For these applications, one of their most attractive features is the format: 'on this condition, do that' (Davis and King 1977). It is essentially the same feature, that of choice restricted by previous choice, that we take to be one of the most valuable aspects of networks for the purposes of qualitative analysis.

7.5 USING NETS TO REPRESENT

Ultimately because of the power and generality of the graph concept (7.4.1) the great majority of pictures one comes across which purport to show some complex structure do it with some kind of net. The present section shows how our networks relate to some of the various kinds of net that have been used by others.

One large family of such nets are usually called semantic networks, the term deriving from Quillian (1968). Quillian wanted to incorporate some significant part of the common dictionary knowledge of people in a computer system, and did so by a network in which the nodes were words, and the links were a small number of essentially logical types. His links were essentially:

'is a case of'
'is modified by'
'or'
'and'

'relation R relates X to Y'
'look further under the heading X'.

Quillian's early work encoded in this way some 850 words of Basic English, and the programme accepted requests for comparisons of pairs of words. It responded to such a request with something like:

compare CRY & COMFORT:
To cry is among other things to make a sad sound
To comfort can be to make something less sad

compare PLANT & LIVE:
A plant is a live structure which gets food from air.
This food is stuff which beings have to take into themselves to keep alive.

This early work has been much developed (see e.g. Findler 1979), and there has been much debate as to just what, and how many, kinds of linkage such a network ought to have (Woods 1975). An example given by Shapiro (1979) is shown in Figure 7.7.

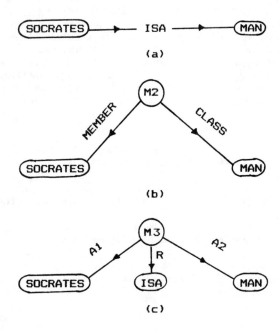

Figure 7.7   Three kinds of linking
for the same relation

In Figure 7.7(a) the link 'is a case of' is used, so that the relation itself is not explicitly represented, merely used. In (b) there is a node representing the member-class relation. In (c) the representation is yet more abstract, with a node for any binary relation, connected to SOCRATES and MAN so as to show that SOCRATES is the first term of the relation IS A whose second term is MAN. The circuitousness of the English reflects the explicitness of the representation, and its corresponding abstraction.

Systemic networks in our use of them employ very few and very abstract linkage resources. As mentioned elsewhere, and as shown in Section 7.4 a systemic network uses one type of link - essentially an arrow or pointer - and three types of abstract node, namely a node containing a terminal, and nodes containing non-terminals from which one either exits by one or by all paths offered. The interpretations given to these types are:

> further described by this term
> one of the following kinds
> must be described on all the following dimensions

Clearly, the less abstract and more particular the links available are made, the simpler the resulting net and the plainer the way the net says what it has to say. But, in payment, the more specific the links are, the more of them one needs, and the more specialised any one set of them will tend to be. Thus a link such as 'is a friend of' could greatly simplify a net to deal with relations between people, but be useless for other purposes. In analysis with systemic networks, essentially everything has to go into the terms themselves, including all the relations as well as the 'objects' standing in those relations. We take this in the end to be a virtue, on the grounds of wide applicability, explicitness and epistemological neutrality.

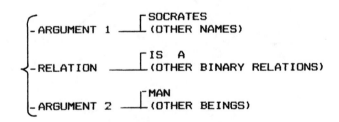

Figure 7.8   Network version of
              Figure 7.7(c)

The interested reader may wish to pursue the comparison by looking at other examples in the literature, such as the systems of Schank (Schank 1973) or of Minsky (Minsky 1974, Roberts and Goldstein 1977). Schank develops a set of abstract 'cases' intended to reflect all the fundamental kinds of connection between things one might want to talk about. Minsky suggests 'frames': a frame being a complex node designed to contain all the information one might normally have, especially that which one usually takes for granted, about an object.

One may regard such possibilities as lying on a spectrum, from rich and complex nodes (such as frames) joined by very few (perhaps just one) kinds of link, to very simple nodes joined by a great variety of links. A systemic network tries to do both at the same time, by making what might be a wide variety of links into terms of the network itself, and employing as actual links only the few very abstract ones offered by the network notation. Thus a network version of Figure 7.7(c) might look like Figure 7.8.

It follows that one must look amongst the terms of a network both for the relations and objects related: that indeed they are on a par in this form of representation, with the advantage that relations of relations are as easy to express as relations of objects. What we have called the managerial parts of networks are generally the broad, often simple, structuring relations amongst the things described.

Chapter 8

CONCLUDING QUESTIONS AND PROBLEMS

To have any dealings with qualitative data, in whatever field of research, is inevitably to confront large and long-standing problems concerning its nature, sources, interpretation, analysis and legitimacy. One cannot avoid questions that have troubled philosophers, sociologists, psychologists and others beside; questions around which there exists a substantial literature reflecting the very varied perspectives from which such scholars have approached the issues. To attempt to recapitulate such arguments here would be impossible, but it is nevertheless necessary to touch on some, where they are particularly important for analysis using networks.

In addressing a number of such fundamental questions and problems, we shall start from the assumption that one already has something one is prepared to count as 'data', and that one has some coherent view or other of its nature and standing. This is of course not merely a large assumption; indeed it could be seen as under-cutting all the essential difficulties. However, we believe that we have to take the view, for our present purposes, that it is not appropriate for us to attempt to tell researchers from differing disciplines or persuasions how they ought to or might regard their data. At the same time, we would wish to avoid any suggestion that the use of networks is a purely 'technical' affair, independent of deep differences about the nature of the problem concerned. Far from it: no analysis can avoid taking some fundamental position. An example of the kind of discussion which ought to inform the use of networks might, in sociologically oriented work, be the symposium report 'The Analysis of Qualitative Data' (Ed. Blaxter 1979) which reviews arguments about the nature of data from various standpoints, in relation to a number of case studies, tracing the arguments to their major sources.

Sections 8.1 and 8.2 divide some concluding questions and problems into two groups: those which concern when or whether the use of networks might be appropriate or not (8.1) and those about how to decide on the merits or demerits of a given network (8.2). Section 8.3 briefly refers to some of the deeply problematic issues mentioned above, and states some positions. Section 8.4 concludes with a short discussion of possible future uses of the methodology.

8.1 WHY, WHEN AND WHETHER TO USE NETWORKS?

Is there anything special about networks as an analytic tool?   What might they buy me, and what price may I find I have paid?   Do they commit me to some methodological position: if so, do I like it?   Are there kinds of problem to which they are suited or unsuited?.

   If I want to develop a network, where is it to come from?   What view of data will it or ought it to presuppose?   Seen as a net, what kind of fish can it catch?.

   These and related questions are discussed here.   In their nature, not all can be answered definitively, but in such cases we have tried to say why it is hard to give a clear answer.

8.1.1   The Given Versus the Problematic

Much depends whether what is to go into a network can be taken as given, or is problematic.   Consider two possible examples: say a description of syllabus content and a description of the relevance of curriculum experiences to everyday concerns.   It is possible (though not obvious) that the terms in the first case could be taken as they stand, without question, from (say) published documents.   It seems certain, however, that in the second case the terms in which to provide a description would be initially quite unclear.

   The first case would then be one of re-representing as a network the given structure of the syllabus.   To be sure, this might not be easy and might throw up a host of difficulties.   The syllabus may leave much implicit, or have little evident structure.   But in many cases, a fair network could be worked out just from the divisions of topics and abilities in the material itself.   In the second case, much of the problem would be to define the problem.   It is likely that what would count as 'relevant' and why, or what kinds of 'experiences' to identify, would all be problematic.   Supposing for the sake of argument that this is how things are, then so far as the use of networks is concerned, the two problems look very different. The first is almost a technical job, simply exploiting the notation to represent a structure.   The second case, unlike the first, is one of not knowing what to put in a network, as opposed to knowing what to put in but not knowing quite where or how.   The very terms or categories are problematic: any proposed category presupposes a whole way of looking at the data whose value is itself in question; equally any way of thinking about the data suggests categories about which one has doubts.   Even what counts as data may be at issue.

   If we consider the examples in Chapter 3, we see that few are so extreme, but that nevertheless the contrast is useful.   Example 8, on representing the content of physics questions, is perhaps the nearest to the first case, basically because the content derives both from an already well-structured subject matter and from a teaching course in which the 'architecture' of that subject matter has been given a certain form.   In a general sense, this network operates within a fairly strong 'theory' of its content.

By contrast, Example 1, concerning students' reactions, is much more nearly like the second, problematic, case. A critique of this network and its encoding of data could well be about what it does: its terms and their connections can all be put in doubt. It is worth noting that different parts of this network rely on underlying ideas or 'theories' of very different kinds and status. Part uses the relatively unproblematic everyday commonsense 'theory' that the student's human universe consists of self and others , the latter divided into teachers and peers. Even so, it is possible to imagine different approaches perhaps analysing in terms of basic kinds of interaction instead of in kinds of person. Other parts, notably that describing feelings, rely at least to a degree on broad psychological ideas, particularly distinctions such as those concerning feelings about oneself with feelings of involvement beyond oneself, and again between feelings of desire and obligation. Such an analysis could be attacked either for being too superficial or for being too detached from everyday perception.

Other examples belong to neither extreme. In Example 4, Nancy Johnson is at pains to insist that she did not want to represent a child's mathematical knowledge in terms given either by mathematics or pedagogy, but in terms - therefore problematic - proper to the child. So she makes this a case of the second kind, by decision. However, and not unreasonably, much of her network is indeed related to existing, taken-as-given terms such as adding and multiplying. The reason, and a good one, is that the child is interacting with a world in which these terms are given, and has taken some of them on board. In the limit, cases of the second kind raise all those fundamental questions about what counts as data, about what a theory ought to be like, about where theories come from and how they are tested or validated (or whether they can be); indeed about what it is to 'do research'.

The point we wish to make here is that the decision to use a network for analysis is rather little affected by whatever commitments one has to answers to such questions. The network one actually produces, by contrast, will be loaded with such baggage: it cannot escape being so. Even open-minded neutrality towards 'what is in the data' is a strong epistemological commitment of a kind, sometimes the stronger for its presuppositions being implicit or unconscious. To use a network involves mainly holding that the data can and should be describable from some point of view, in terms more general and less particular than the data itself. It does not involve holding any special view about the nature of that description.

8.1.2 The Development of Categories

Nobody looking at a network would imagine that it sprang fully formed into the analyst's mind. Whilst larger issues of the relation of theory and data are discussed later (8.3) we here consider the nature of the interplay between network and data in the development of a network.

Whether for use in a network, or not, the development of any descriptive category usually means moving backwards and forwards between data and description. Some initial cluster of items of data is tentatively thought of as describable by some category label, probably rather ill-defined. Other cases are sought, and out of trying to decide whether they fall in that category or not, the definition of the category changes. Sometimes, the tentative original category has to be discarded, when a lack of sense in its original conception becomes plain. Sometimes the development is more straightforward, consisting mostly of refinement and clarification of criteria for inclusion.

Thus far, there is nothing special about networks involved, and indeed many of the issues concerning the sources of, criteria for, and development of category schemes are common to many kinds of qualitative analysis. All have in common that one or more **category names** are given to **sets of instances,** with **defining criteria** sought which decide whether a new instance belongs to the named set or not. The categories may, or may not, reflect some explicit theory about the data; where it is not explicit, there will always be some idea, perhaps intuitive, about 'how things are'. There may be a phase in which category definitions are basically ostensive; that is, simply point to a current set of instances, so that the definition in essence says no more than 'things like these'. One can rarely afford to be content with that, because a category remains private if how a likeness is to be recognised cannot be explained. If there is a difference in working with networks, it is that a network presents categories ordered in delicacy, and structured by a pattern of co-selections.

As was mentioned in Chapter 4, one has broadly speaking two choices in starting a network; to begin with the most delicate features, close to the data, and to attempt to combine them into less delicate groups, or to begin with the least delicate features indicating the main outlines of a descriptive scheme, and to refine them towards the more delicate end until one gets close enough to what is 'there' in the data. That is, roughly speaking, one can work 'bottom up' or 'top down'.

In a general way, if one is working top down, terms in a network are more likely to reflect some theoretical position concerning how to think about the data. Thus what would best begin a set of distinctions about students' motivation could well be deeply influenced by what kind of thing one took 'motivation' to be; what appeared at the topmost level in a network concerning classroom interactions would be likely to vary a great deal depending on the stance one was taking about what is important in the classroom. The network in the example of childrens' classifications (Example 3.2) explicitly derives from a particular sociological theory.

At the same time, such least delicate terms will be at several removes from the data. One may have, for example, a general distinction between (say) 'problem solving' and 'solution evaluation' in problem solving studies, or one between 'interactive' and 'non-interactive' classroom events, but these connect as yet only tenuously with actual observations such as a student writing something on paper or a class doing something with a teacher.

It is at the most delicate end of the network that terms correspond closely to the more immediate, perhaps even 'obvious', sometimes superficial aspects of data. Working bottom up, one can often readily think of a considerable number of things to say about the data, at that level. The problem is then that how these link together, or what larger frameworks they presuppose, is often far from clear. It may well be that things which strike one quite forcibly about particular items of data are hard to fit together into a sensible whole. It is our experience that often a network is developed from both ends at once, and there are good reasons why this is so. The very formulation of the research problem presupposes some general ways of looking at things, embodied in its purpose and conception. Thus in the example concerning students' reactions (Example 3.1) given the pragmatic origin and function of the study, such main aspects as the nature of the situation described by the student, the reactions it evoked and the reasons for those reactions could hardly have been avoided. However, there will often also be delicate features one wants to include in a description, which do not fit into a planned mould. So thinking about the bottom end of the network, will come to influence thinking about the top end. Nor, of course, is this merely an unhappy consequence of the complexity of real data, but can and often should be the outcome of deliberately looking at data for surprises; for just that which challenges an old conception or suggests a new one.

For these kinds of reasons, we find that much of the work in building networks goes into developing the middle connecting levels of delicacy. The process is often like first having some general idea and then noticing a conflicting or confirming detail, or first being struck by particulars and getting from them some large but unclear insight, followed by a struggle to link the two. So filling out the middle of the network is in part at least the business of filling out and connecting together one's intuitions, or of elaborating and clarifying a few broad notions into their many recognisable manifestations.

8.1.3 Heuristic Uses of Networks

As several examples in Chapter 3 show, a network can on a single page store and display a collection of related categories, each 'obvious' enough in itself, but whose interdependence would otherwise be difficult to manage, remember or communicate. Usefully on occasions networks can be used to represent complex data structures which, in this way, can be more easily remembered or more efficiently communicated. For example, details of an experimental design with several groups of subjects, a number of treatments and associated variables, can be dealt with through a network, where a diagrammatic representation might need more than three dimensions. Thus in Example 3.6, on problem solving processes, even the problem of identifying chemical quantities used in a calculation proved tedious and liable to be left incomplete without some such notation.

When the problem is a deep uncertainty about what should go into the description at all, there are certain dangers in using networks. It is all too easy to forget that elaborating a bad idea does not improve it. One can set up an initial, inevitably dubious scheme, and then patch it up or repair it with more and more detail, instead of diagnosing what is structurally or conceptually wrong with it, throwing it away, and starting again from a new angle informed by that diagnosis. It is no less easy to fall into the trap of supposing that a mass of complex detail, all well-captured, adds up to an insight. Examples where this is a clear danger are those on problem solving (Example 3.6) and on students' reactions (Example 3.1.). In both, particularly the first, a detailed account of small scale events is relied on to enable one to see significant patterns at a later stage of further analysis. Nothing in using networks assures the safety of such reliance.

More positively, in such problematic cases, a network is at least a useful heuristic device for inspecting and considering one's current descriptive scheme. The very baldness and compactness of the network sets out the scheme with all its inadequacies. Our experience here is that, before starting a network, one often has the feeling of possessing a large, rich and sensitive, albeit not yet quite clearly formulated set of thoughts about the data, but that when one does come to write it out as a network, what strikes one most at first is its paucity, naivety and inner contradictions. At the least, this can act as a strong stimulus to do better, and the structured but extendable or modifiable form a network does allow new ideas to be incorporated relatively easily.

8.1.4 Finiteness and Counting

In the end, a network is a finite system. It assigns a limited description, taken from definite choices between a finite number of terms, to items of data. This is often, and rightly, a source of unease.

A simple but real unease is the feeling that most sets of distinctions are like a continuous spectrum, not a few different colours. However, a system in a network can have as many distinctions as the case calls for, which one can also reliably distinguish. In fact, even though one might want to say that there are tens, or hundreds, of shades of reaction from liking to disliking, or from remembering to not remembering, the data and the subtlety of one's perceptions rarely support more than a few. It may also be that subtlety is better caught by describing some co-selectable qualifying features rather than by finer shading of choices.

In any case, description has to end somewhere. The subtlest, most allusive account, though it may serve better than a network for some purposes, is still finite, though enriched and given a sense of depth by the resonances and associations it suggests to the reader

187

(which, it should be remembered, are not decided by the analyst). So, whilst in no way claiming that a network is never too restrictive or too clumsy a tool, we do want to say that initial and understandable fears of this kind are often much less well-founded than they appear.

Being finite, and so assigning in principle the same description to more than one item of data, a network treats some things which are different as the same, for the purpose in hand. Here network analysis stands somewhere between the nomothetic and the ideographic. That is, on the one hand it is not that position which describes things broadly and simply (under versus over-achievers, introverted versus extroverted, task-oriented versus reward-oriented) and proceeds forthwith to count cases. On the other hand, it does not treat every case as individual, to be described solely in its own terms.

A network allows the counting of cases described in the same way, or whose descriptions contain the same coded terms. We thus have to face the important question of when it is justifiable to count. To count is to treat things as being alike for a given purpose; to act as if two items are twice as many as one. (Clearly bigamy is not to have twice as many wives in the same way as to have two good friends is to be doubly befriended).

In the example of students' reactions (Example 3.1) feelings at the broad level of 'good' or 'bad' were in fact counted in further analysis, and were related to, for example, year of study and type of story. In the example of pupils' comments on one another (Example 3.5) categorised comments such as 'fun' were counted and related to membership or non-membership of cliques, and to gender. It must be right to regard this as problematic. On the other hand, results which look meaningful have emerged.

If one wants to use a network analysis to count features, the task of constructing the network is then to construct countable features; to identify descriptive labels which, for the purpose in hand, treat as similar things one has some justification for treating in that way. There can rarely be clinching arguments for or evidence of similarity but at least one should ensure that possible counter-arguments have been considered. For example, in the case of perceptions of standards implied by APU items (Example 3.3) it might be open to doubt whether an 'easy' rating by a school teacher ought to be counted as equivalent to the same rating given by an industrialist.

A network, of course, may have little or nothing to do with counting. The description of one child's mathematical knowledge (Example 3.4), for instance, has no concern with saying whether one feature arises more often than another. The question simply does not arise. A study of classroom language might concern itself solely with possible kinds of utterance, and not at all with relative frequency, but more likely it might take it as important first to get a good analysis of possible utterances and then later to look at style. Or, one may have a network designed for counting, and then in using it, elaborate or redefine some of the possibilities. Janet Holland (Example 3.2) gives an example of this kind of process, modifying the network previously set up to describe children's classifications of food items, without departing from its main outlines.

We do not have any special preference for rendering qualitative data in a numerical form. It is simply that the possibility exists on occasion, and needs to be considered in relation to the problem in hand with some caution, tact and good sense.

8.2 WHAT MAKES A GOOD NETWORK?

A description can obviously be better or worse; more faithful or less, over- or under- detailed, clearer or less clear. Since a network and any associated code exist for the purpose of describing data, we have to consider by what standards and in what ways network descriptions might fairly be judged.

Much of what there is to say necessarily holds for many kinds - perhaps for any kind - of qualitative analysis, and so can be said briefly. We shall primarily try to bring out those features which are particular to the use of networks.

However, there cannot be one overall account of criteria for judging the merits of network and code, for the reason that networks can be used within a wide range of kinds of research, so diverse that problems even of what constitutes a valid result change from one kind to another. Thus what may look like a practical problem of checking a network against relevant criteria is nothing of the kind; rather we have to consider how to judge networks from a very general position which accepts that each user will be defining his or her own terms of reference.

Thus for the present discussion we take the following relativist and eclectic point of view.

a network is to be judged within the terms set by the mode of research within which it is embedded.

a network gives a description of data intended by the analyst, and is to be judged by how well it fulfills the analyst's intentions, not (for our purpose) by what one may think of them.

we have too little experience of using networks, and their uses range too widely, for it to be reasonable to offer more than suggestive guidelines, as opposed to prescriptions.

Any system of description needs to be in some sense valid and reliable. 'Validity' means something like being appropriate in kind, and - within that kind - sufficiently complete and faithful. 'Reliability' means something like a good enough degree of agreement between people as to how to use the system to describe data.

It is worth asking what properties one would reasonably expect any description to have. A description should surely be clear, and be complete enough for its purpose: it ought not to leave obvious relevant holes. It should be self-consistent, not allowing self-contradictory or absurd accounts of things. Its level or grain of detail should match the task, given that it is best if concise. What it says needs to be understandable and learnable: if not it probably serves more to persuade or impress than to describe. None of these features should lead, if it can be avoided, to clumsiness of expression - a good description expresses its account well as well as correctly. It must by some standards be fitting: give a faithful rather than a distorted picture. And finally, one would usually like it in some significant sense to transcend the original: to describe data as something, not merely to repeat or copy it.

We shall look at criteria for networks in these terms.

8.2.1 Completeness

It would clearly count against the network of Example 3.4 if it left out some important dimension of the child's mathematical knowledge. It would count against that of Example 3.7 if it failed to capture something of pupils' ideas of force. It would count against that of Example 3.5 if it missed describing interesting comments of one child on another.

A first primitive test for any network is whether all items of data are given reasonable descriptions. Elementary though the requirement is, it is in practice one of the hardest to satisfy as a network is developed. It is all too common for a network, laboured over for some time, to fail on the very next batch of data, and such failures are one of the main sources for further development, through a diagnosis of the reasons for the failure. In Example 3.1 Joan Bliss describes how the network for students' reactions failed to include even so simple a matter as the student reacting to an experiment not working, in that case because the network had been developed with interpersonal interactions too strongly in mind.

How far one goes in requiring completeness must depend on the purpose in hand and on the degree to which one holds that the data deserves an exhaustive description. A good example of insistence on completeness is Sinclair and Coulthard's account (not in network terms) of classroom discourse, described in Chapter 6. True to their linguistic orientation, they would regard an element of discourse not described within a systematic scheme, and so treated as 'accident' - not rule governed - as an important defect. Janet Holland's account in Example 3.2 shows how an initial reasonably satisfactory network was extended to make it account for more material than before.

It is not enough to ask that the data, as seen through the current descriptive scheme, be all described. What one can see depends on the spectacles one wears, and it may be important to ask whether there are distinctions, predictable from theory or even commonsense, that ought to be included in a network. If the analyst starts mainly from the data - bottom-up in the terms of section 8.1.2 - there may be a view of the data that is altogether missed.

Paradoxically networks, unlike other category schemes, are somewhat prone to generate descriptions of things that are not in the data. That is, a network may have paradigms which have no instances in data. To take a simple case, it can easily be that the network in Example 3.8 describing examination items produces 'items' that happen never to have been written - there may no cases of questions about, say, alternating currents. It may be that this is perfectly in order: that the missing instances are entirely reasonable paradigms whose lack of instantiation is in itself good information (it might lead to such questions being written). In Example 3.6, in the part of the network describing chemical quantities used in solving a problem, the absence of some quantities from any actual solution could be worth noting. Everything here depends on the relevant paradigms being quite natural and reasonable within the descriptive framework adopted.

Such cases need careful examination, of course. A network can express the absence of something in two ways: by including it as a paradigm which is instantiated with zero frequency, or by excluding it as a paradigm. The choice between the two is important but not easy to make. Suppose that in some study like that of Mike Watts (Example 3.7) children had thought of energy and force as 'in' some objects and as 'acting on' others, but that there were some objects (such as golfballs) for which both possibilities occurred and others (such as tables) for which only one occurred. Would it be best to make the network allow it for tables and then say that the case does not occur? Insofar as the absence of a combination seems most like a structural feature, it seems best to make the network disallow it. By comparison, in Example 3.2, since context-bound conceptualisations are expected by the underlying theory, it would seem best to have them in the network even if, on some test material, there had been no cases of them.

8.2.2 Consistency

It is not excluded that the possibilities allowed by a network are incoherent or inconsistent. It would seem easy, as well as obviously necessary, to avoid such inconsistency, but this is sometimes less simple than it sounds.

A common case of the difficulty is rather trivial. The network described by Paul Black in Example 3.7 is intended to yield descriptive strings for problem-solving steps, each described along several rather general dimensions, such as PURPOSE, ACTION, etc. Now some of the specific, more delicate possibilities under each dimension do not make sense in combination. Thus the system which allows the student to READ the PROBLEM also 'allows' him to READ the SOLUTION. The case is relatively trivial, because the main aim of the network is to include a large number of possibilities in as simple a way as possible, and provided that nobody interprets the absence of students reading the solution as informative in any way, no harm will be done.

On the other hand, one ought to regard such possibilities as a warning that the network structure does not yet in itself faithfully reflect the structure of actual alternatives.

One should perhaps distinguish counterfactual possibilities, such as snowfall in high summer, from self-contradictory ones such as being awake while asleep; clearly the second are the more problematic. Logical difficulties of this kind tend to arise in the development of a network when two dimensions or aspects, thought of as different but in fact related, are introduced. Thus in one early version of a network about problem solving (not that of Example 3.6) distinctions in one part of the network concerned the manner of approach to a problem, as direct, tentative or speculative, while distinctions elsewhere, co-occurring with the first, concerned the mode of operation of the student, as actual or hypothetical. Although various combinations made good sense, even including making an actual calculation as part of a speculative approach, or hypothesising as part of a direct attempt to get the solution, the two sets of distinctions were uncomfortably close.

The notion of consistency must not be misunderstood. Nothing prevents people in real life behaving or thinking inconsistently, and it may be a legitimate goal of a network to describe such self-contradiction. Obvious examples are those concerned with children's conceptions (Examples 3.4 and 3.7). The point is merely that the description should not contradict itself.

8.2.3 Sufficiency of Detail

One particular advantage of networks is the ability of the analyst to add to, or to reduce, the delicacy of description. There can clearly be no general rules about how far to go, except that there can be no sense in making fine distinctions that are in fact too fine to be reliably distinguished.

It fairly often turns out to be the case that one person analysing data with a network pushes distinctions a little beyond what is reasonable, no doubt because someone developing a network comes to know the data very well and can readily see fine detail in it. An advantage of networks is that if the most delicate distinctions are well-grouped under less delicate ones, a second person can often agree fairly easily about the less delicate terms to choose, while being unsure about the most delicate. Thus in the network describing feelings in Example 3.1, it could well be difficult for a second person to be sure if a feeling expressed in a transcript should count as relatively intense or not, while finding it easy to agree that it was at least a case of satisfaction.

It follows that the reliability of a network will vary from place to place, in the sense that two or more coders will agree better about some terms than others. It is likely that agreement will be better as one moves up to less delicate terms.

Reliability apart, the detail one needs to give in a network must be a function of the quality of data and the purpose of the analysis. Thus in Example 3.5, Martin Monk was working with data consisting of a few written words about each child, so that any great delicacy of description of reactions could not have been supported by evidence.

The question of how detailed a description to give is, of course, endemic in all qualitative analysis. It is as easy to be tempted into excessive minutae as into empty generalities. It is important, however, to distinguish the functions of network analysis from those of reportage: the network description of a piece of data looks at it by comparison with the rest of the data, via contrasts of meaning relating to the whole, whereas reportage will usually serve the different function of 'bringing to life' something individual about one item of data.

8.2.4 Learnability

An 'analysis' of data is, by definition, an attempt to make public some perceptions of the data, at least if one is concerned with research. Now qualitative data often has the property that a good deal of private effort is required even to assimilate it, let alone find ways of characterising it. It follows that communicating the terms of the analysis to others is likely to be non-trivial, except in the rare case that the data can be analysed in already well-known terms. Yet communicating the analysis is central; it is logically prior to any notion of reliability, as it is to any notion of comparing results. So we shall discuss reliability from this standpoint.

Much hinges on whether networks are relatively easy or hard to teach to others. In this respect we do think that they have certain advantages over some other kinds of categorisation, particularly when one has to have complex over-lapping categories. It is helpful that terms get much of their meaning by contrast with the others against which they contrast. It is also helpful that properties of terms are inherited back up a tree, so that part of the meaning of a term can be sought amongst related distinctions. Notice that Janet Holland's Example 3.2 is precisely a case of learning a category system through learning a network. The system she had to learn, and then elaborated, is not perhaps very formidable, though in fact it does contain some 21 different end-categories, which presented as a list with extended descriptions might well look much more complex than it appears as a network.

It also seems to us to help that the network displays the structure and relation of descriptive terms diagramatically rather than in the form of sentences with logical connectives. One can see which terms are subordinate to which others, which represent co-existing aspects, and so on, with rather little difficulty.

However, an analysis may be difficult to teach and learn, not because of its complexity or subtlety, but because it is confused or ill-chosen. It is, of course, just such problems that checks on reliability are needed to detect. Here we tend to find that different parts of a given network present widely differing difficulties. One part may be uncontroversial; easy to learn and use. Another may seem clear but one finds on checking that coders are using it inconsistently. Here one can always blame the training process, but at some point one has to consider reforming the network. Yet another part may be excessively hard to learn, seeming to the trainee like an incommunicable private perception of the writer of the network. Such problems exist in the checking or reliability of any coding scheme, of course, and if networks are special in any way it is merely by handling considerable complexity in a structured way which can be tackled piecemeal.

8.2.5 Testability

A network may claim no more than to be a reasonably accurate record of things or events for a purpose. By contrast a network may derive, not so much from data, but from a theoretical position, as discussed previously (Sections 8.1.1, 8.1.2).

These uses of networks relate differently to the issue of testability, whether of testing a network as a 'theory' against data, or of testing data against a 'theory' or expectation via a network.

Perhaps the simplest case is when the same network is used to give descriptions to data in two or more sub-samples, and one asks whether the number and pattern of cases is the same or not. Thus it makes perfectly good sense to use the network in Example 3.8 to check if the subject matter balance of examinations composed from items changes over the years. Here the network is just a device for managing a complex comparison.

Another kind of test, this time more a test of the network, would be to see if a description produced for one group was extendable to other groups, modifiable by circumstances and so on. It makes sense to ask if different teaching would influence the dynamical ideas Mike Watts finds children to have. These are at least in some sense tests of the network, because they inspect the extent to which it is generalisable or is more than the artefact of one researcher's perception of the data.

If the paradigms of a network are intended to make a strong assertion about the nature of the data, then further data may put the network itself to the test. Either the data can be represented by the paradigms, or it cannot. If not, it will usually be the case that the network can be modified so as to avoid such difficulties, and this is precisely what happens in the development of a network. It seems to follow that a network cannot be put to a final test, since there is always the possibility of altering it, and one might want to argue this as a significant defect, on the grounds that a descriptive system which cannot be tested because it can always be changed, has in the end little substance.

Our view is that one must not deny the difficulty, and that one needs to be continually aware of the danger that what seems like an improvement may be more nearly an ad-hoc modification. But, at the same time, too much insistence on rigid hypotheses, not to be modified in the light of data, is at the end of the day only an insistence that research must succeed or fail at the first attempt.

8.2.6   Expressiveness and Persuasiveness

The expressions which describe data are some form of code deriving from a selection of terms in a network. Pieces of code can have any relation, even an arbitrary one, to network terms;   as we said in Chapter 2, network terms are **realised** in code according to **realisation rules** chosen by the analyst.

The code may be chosen so as to be as brief as possible, as in Example 3.2 where the need is simply to count kinds of conceptualisation, or as in Example 3.5 where reasonably straightforward kinds of categorisation of children's comments are to be counted. The rules for constructing code may, however, deserve to be a good deal more elaborate, especially if further analysis will be done by looking at the codes. Thus in the study of students' reactions (Example 3.1) and in the study of problem solving (Example 3.6) coding rules were exploited to generate strings of code in a kind of pseudo-English which aids comprehension of the underlying pattern of choice in the network.

It is important to realise that this can be overdone. Helpful as the choice of an expressive coding word or neat use of indentation or brackets may be, the code actually says no more than the network distinguishes.   It is in the network, not in any subtle choice of expression, that the analytic distinctions are made.   So, if a network distinguishes (say) three kinds of school, coded expressions which (through their English meaning) suggest contrasts with half a dozen types, do no more analytic work than would cruder expressions.

Having stated the danger, there is surely much to be said for a method of analysis and coding which can, if required, encode data in a form something like a clause of a natural language, at least in that doing so can make the learning of a scheme and testing its reliability less tiresome.   It may also make it easier to look for and see patterns in codes - it must be simpler to scan expressions like TEACHER SEEMED INTERESTED or FIRST CALCULATED MASS OF GAS than more arbitrary ones.

Let us turn briefly to a related, but deep and difficult point: the legitimacy or otherwise of the persuasive element in an analysis. It is something of a scientific convention that the 'truth' remains the truth however clumsily told, although much value is also attached even in the 'hardest' of sciences to elegance of reasoning and clarity of perception.   That said, the 'hardest' sciences retain some inherent level at which their discourse has the function of persuasion (as opposed to demonstration):   at the least, of persuasion to look at a question in one way rather than another.

In the social sciences, even at their most quantitative, there is the same need to persuade concerning the fundamental approach (even when the persuasion is done by taking the rightness of the approach totally for granted), and greater difficulty because of the variety of possible competing perspectives.   There are difficulties, not always fully recognised, even in treating a variable as meaning what it seems to mean: whether 'intelligence' operationalised in some way 'measures' intelligence is an obvious case;   whether the 'school attendance rate' indicates the school attendance rate may be no less a problem. Methods of quantitative analysis also invest their expressions with rhetorical as well as with technical force; the phrase 'percentage of variance explained by heredity' conveys that the problem is well modelled in terms of partitioning variance, when in fact it might not be.

In qualitative analysis, the same problems are further compounded, and are indeed the reason why many treat it with extreme caution. It is all too evident that to label children as 'under-achieving' or 'over-achieving' is to do much more than to merely describe. The examples in Chapter 3 reveal the problem in a variety of ways at a variety of levels. Even the 'neutral' terms taken from physics to describe examination items (Example 3.8) presume that such terms are appropriate. More obviously problematic are such cases as some perceptions of children's performance or children's ideas about force (Examples 3.3 and 3.7).

The difficulty is transparently present in analysis using networks because the network scheme provides no initial, taken-as-given, kind of content. Just as a logic presumes nothing about what will be said in that logic, so a network leaves everything to be said by the analyst, in the choice of network terms and their possible combinations.

A network analysis does, however, open the possibility of connecting terms of analysis rather directly to items of data, through the concept of increasing delicacy. One who wants to challenge the fitness of a description can be shown in some detail how it related to items of data, and can also, because the network displays all the descriptive possibilities, examine and challenge their basis. So, although a network analysis does not, and never could, escape the fact that the foundations of an analysis are always problematic, those foundations are to a considerable degree open to inspection. The flaws tend to be all too visible.

8.2.7 The Finished Network

The question whether a network is as good as it could be can hardly have an answer, save in practical terms that enough effort seems to have been expended on it for the purpose in hand. Networks, like poems, are abandoned rather than finished. We have already discussed some of the criteria by which a network might be judged to have been improved.

For the purposes of the present book, concerned with the use of networks in general terms and not with specific applications except as needed examples of general problems, we accept (as stated at the beginning of Section 8.2) that each network has to be judged in the analyst's own terms. Those terms will include ways of deciding whether what the network does, in the framework of the domain of application, looks interesting, important and novel.

Nothing in the technique of using networks can tell one how to achieve those ends; indeed it is important not to be dazzled by technique into thinking that more has been achieved than has really been. If what is in a network has value, it all comes from and depends on the qualities of the person who put it there, or of those others whose previous ideas it puts to use. No network is better than its authors.

8.3 THEORY AND DATA

Working with networks, as in any research, one continually confronts questions of the relation of theory and data. Amongst them are all those about the ways in which theory could (or could not) in some sense arise from inspecting data, all those about how a theory determines the nature of data collection and its interpretation, all those about whether - (and if so, how) - data can put theory to some kind of test, and - crucial in the social sciences - all those questions about the solidity, standing, 'hardness' or 'softness' of data and the extent to which 'data' itself is a problematic notion. As a technique, analysis using networks does not, and could not, solve any of these fundamental questions, though it may make some more prominent than others.

We do not regard the network notation method as forcing one into any very narrowly defined theoretical framework. One person's network can readily contain terms another would think to be highly problematic, but this would be an argument about substance, not about the form of its expression in a network. Indeed, the examples in Chapter 3 range over a wide variety of kinds of subject matter, and include cases where the underlying philosophical positions taken differ quite markedly.

This is not the place for an essay on the sources of theory; on inductivism versus hypothetico-deductivism, on the problematic versus the taken-for-granted or (in Blumer's (1954) terms) on sensitising versus definitive concepts. Our own rather conventional position is that any analysis of data is the analyst's responsibility, being unavoidably his or her own perception of data. And every perception of data is a perception through some idea about the data, some previous 'theory' of it. The 'theory' is not necessarily very good, deep, profound or clear: it may be little more than commonsense (and for that reason the harder to notice). Even what counts as 'data' depends on one's theory, point of view, or perspective.

Having said this, it seems to us no less important to insist that this does not mean that there is no sense in the closely attentive, open-minded inspection of data to 'find what is to be found'. There is every reason to comb data as deeply and as 'neutrally' as possible, so as to allow oneself to be struck by those things which grate on, run counter to, or seem odd in the light of one's preconceptions. Thus although a network cannot be 'derived from' the data, there is a different and important sense in which it can and should be, in that it embodies a new view of data mediated by a reconciliation of data and ideas. Here we are saying little more than Glaser and Strauss (1967) whose notion of grounded theory is one of careful and exhaustive dialogue between category and data, inspected as carefully for misfit as for fit.

We also take the conventional view that a theory ought to account for data and fails where it does not; that the final test is one against reality, not purely one of elegance of consistency. At the same time, it would be presumptuous to expect too much too soon. Many problems are still at the stage where various ways of looking at them need exploring, not testing. Many are at the stage where the problem is what the problem is, not what the answer is. Here, and even where one thinks one is further forward, real data has a quirkiness of character and an intransigence that makes it hard to set up any clear test. Theories have a cloudiness that prevents one saying just what they do predict and what not. The advantage that networks offer here is simply to attack some of the difficulties bit by bit, because the power of a network to handle complexity means that not all complexities need to be dealt with at once. The choice, in fact, is not between testing things properly or not at all, but between doing slightly better or doing nothing. Networks offer some help with doing a little better.

It is, of course, sociologists who have given most attention to problems of the nature of theory and data, not least because it is possible to conceive sociology in such radically different senses that the relationships shift markedly when one moves from one perspective to another. A rather full discussion of the analysis of qualitative data with respect to such varying perspectives is given by Halfpenny (1979).

We do not regard network analysis as replacing, though it may sometimes supplement, other kinds of account of qualitative data. A striking example is that of the study of students' reactions (Example 3.1) vital though the network was to master a large bulk of complex and subtle data without losing touch with the detail, no encoded description can have the force of, nor replace the communicative function of the subject's statement of his or her own reality. Thus,

"You make up your own mind, and you do what you want to do within reason. You have done it on your own, and you haven't been told how to do it."

conveys points about freedom and responsibility with a force that those general terms, however accurate, could never deliver. More deeply, when the central task of the research is to understand, to see the world through the eyes of others or to get inside another culture or subculture, then even though a network may have some use, a sharing of that understanding with others is likely to require the full resources of a shared language and culture simply to shake people out of one set of assumptions and into another (see examples in Halliday 1978). In particular, we do not in any way suggest that a network disposes of the work an interpretivist has to do in entering and understanding a realm of meaning, though one can imagine cases where the notation might be a useful aid.

We equally reject any notion, perhaps positivist in inclination, to regard qualitative data as inherently 'soft' and to see networks as a case of trying to 'harden it up'. If the data is in fact soft, no network will stiffen it against criticism. But we do not, as some do, regard qualitative data as necessarily a problem by contrast with 'hard' data, and this view is helped by the way using networks can make the analysis of such data somewhat more feasible, systematic, and publicly describable. It is our experience that the development of a network description can actually help one locate where and why parts of the analysis are more of a problem than others. Some categories, after a struggle, attain reasonably clear and natural definitions, while others do not and remain unclear, awkward or unconvincing, and this may help to identify problem areas either in the data or in its interpretation.

We should perhaps also repeat the point made in Section 8.1.4 that using a network to count features is a matter for decision, and that a network is not to be regarded as a device for rendering countable the uncountable.

Rather, we see networks being used in a variety of ways; as an heuristic device in thinking about an analysis; as charting the stumbling progress through and arriving at an analysis of new and complex data; as a possible expression of a theory of some data; as an attempt to bridge the gap between theory expressed generally and data in its particularity; and as a way to express structures, as well as from time to time a means to aid counting how often something does or does not occur.

This is not to claim that networks are all things to all people. They do, however, leave it pretty much to the analyst how to structure or construe the world he or she is dealing with. They do not force much, if any, pre-determined form onto that structure. They do not hold allegiance to some theory of how things ought to be construed. Networks make one fundamental requirement: that as the analyst one is prepared to say, on whatever grounds, that I propose to count **this** as a case of **that** - to define and hold constant a distinction.

8.4 WHO MIGHT USE NETWORKS?

We believe that the examples in Chapter 3, and the discussion of them in the rest of the book, make a case for a considerable range of applications of the idea in educational research. It is indeed often a characteristic of educational research, concerned as it is with real situations, that the problem is not a lack of contextual information, but difficulty in dealing with it. We hope we have shown that it is at least sometimes possible to exploit networks to master the bulk and complexity of qualitative data, to the point where it becomes amenable to worthwhile analysis.

It seems clear that in the examples we have offered, the fact that most of the work has an educational focus is not essential to deciding the value of the network method. Education is not notably a specialised discipline, requiring special tools of limited use elsewhere. It is rather the reverse, in that educational research is an omnivorous consumer of methodologies developed in other disciplines. Networks are a case in point, adapted from a linguistic source, and used previously in applied linguistics (see Example 3.9). There therefore seems to be no reason why they might not find useful applications in a number of other social sciences, wherever qualitative data has importance.

We can only offer general reasons in support of such a claim, pointing to the sociological and psychological connections of a number of our examples, to the fundamental nature and small number of the formal resources that networks use, and to the flexibility offered in the scale or scope of any analysis. In the previous section we pointed out the absence of theoretical baggage carried by networks, aside from a necessary commitment to well-defined description in some terms or other.

The book, then, offers some experience in the use of network analysis, some material and ideas we have found helpful in coming to terms with it, and some attempt to think through the consequences of applying the method to various sorts of problem. We would not regard the ideas as yet fully formed, and indeed writing the book has thrown up a number of difficulties deserving of further thought and ideas needing further trial by experience. But we do regard the method as a potentially useful addition to the tools of analysis, particularly in helping to bring about a less sharp cleavage between the 'qualitative' and the 'quantitive'. We believe this to be particularly important in educational research, with its characteristically awkward mixture of the two. We hope, then, that the experience and ideas reported here will prove useful to others, in education and perhaps beyond.

Appendix A

BARBARA

The computer program BARBARA was developed by Francois Grize to allow users to store networks, to type in codes expressed in terms of a network and have them checked and stored, and to question the data about the frequency of features or combinations of features.

At the time of writing, versions of the program have been installed at Imperial College London, and at the University of Neuchatel, Switzerland. Both are interactive. An improved version, but in batch-processing form, is available in Neuchatel, and there are plans for an interactive version with the improvements. The program is written in PASCAL. It is fairly fully described in Grize (1981) and further details can be obtained from the author, F. Grize, Universite de Neuchatel, Pierre-a-Mazel 7, 2000 Neuchatel, Switzerland.

A brief outline of the way the program appears to the user follows.

The first requirement is to input the network. If a network has been stored, codes can be input, or code can be added to (or erased from) previously stored code. The program checks the code against the network, and only accepts code that is, in terms of the network, well-formed. Given stored code, one can input requests for numbers of items of data having any defined collection of features from the network, or ask for lists of items with such features.

To input the network, a simple language is used to express the network notation. Figure A1 shows an arbitrary network and the corresponding description given to BARBARA.

Codes are input as a sequence of symbols from the network, with an identifier for each item of data. Thus one might, for items described by the network of Figure A1, type:

```
ITEM5 = J G
ITEM6 = D E Y
```

It is also possible, but not obligatory, to include non-terminals in the code, with appropriate bracketing, as in:

```
ITEM5 = S( A ( C (J))  B (F ( G  )))
```

Whether non-terminals are included or not, the program checks through the code and notes every occurrence, explicit or implied, of any term. Thus ITEM 5 would later appear in any list of items having the features C, F, C AND F, etc. If the code is ill-formed (perhaps by omitting a required choice of term or by having a combination of terms not allowed by the network) a diagnostic message is provided.

Further simple commands allow questioning of the data:

LIST (combination of terms)   and   NUM (combination of terms)

produce respectively the list of identifiers of items and the number of items having the combination of terms specified in their arguments. The combination can be any Boolean combination of network terms specifiable by the connectives AND, OR, and NOT, such as (J AND NOT (Z) OR (K AND F)). Cross-tabulations can be obtained using:

TAB (first list of terms, second list of terms)

The two lists of terms to be cross-tabulated can contain single terms from the network, Boolean combinations as above, or be the implied list of all terminals reachable from a given non-terminal, using the form TER(non-terminal).

Recent improvements include allowing one to define new names for arbitrary combinations of terms, in the form DEF(new name) = (Boolean combination of terms). The program is being altered to be modular, dividing up its stages of network input, code input and questioning, so that it occupies less space and runs faster.

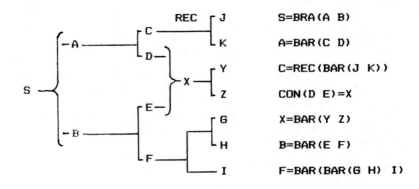

Figure A1   A network and its description to BARBARA

Appendix B

NETWORKS AND CONTINGENCY TABLES

As noted in Chapter 2 and illustrated in some exercises in Chapter 5, a network can be regarded as defining a contingency table. Except for the simplest, such a table will be multidimensional, with arbitrary and varying numbers of categories on each dimension. This Appendix draws attention to modern methods for the analysis of such tables.

Any standard statistical text will describe the chi-squared statistic and its application to 2x2 tables, and may describe extensions to arbitrary two-dimensional (RxC) tables. The essential difficulty in extending chi-squared to the RxC case, or beyond to multidimensional tables, is finding a way of partitioning the total chi-squared into parts attributable to the effects of categories in various dimensions of the table. One possibility is to use a method which possesses a natural extension to many dimensions. Such a method is log-linear analysis.

A very complete discussion of all methods of analysing contingency tables is the text of Bishop, Fienberg and Holland (1975). A book discussing just log-linear analysis in full detail is Fienberg (1978). Both give excellent references to the original literature.

Log linear analysis is available on a number of modern statistical computer packages, including BMD, GLIM, and GENSTAT (though not on current versions of SPSS). It is easy to use, and conceptually quite straightforward.

The fundamental idea of log-linear analysis is that relations in a contingency table are of their nature multiplicative, in that probabilities combine to form joint probabilities by multiplication (e.g. if half of the people are male and a third have brown eyes, then if these traits are independent one sixth of people are brown-eyed males). By working in logarithms, multiplication is transformed into addition, so that one can analyse the transformed table into linearly additive effects ascribed to the categories along various dimensions. Models of the data can be set up and tested, and a best model identified. Correlations between categories show up as the presence of interactions between their effects. A test statistic, distributed asymptotically as chi-squared, is available, which (intuitively) indicates the difference in information carried by the frequencies predicted by the current model and the data frequencies.

REFERENCES

The references are grouped as follows:

1 Work Using Network Analysis for Qualitative Data
2 References for Examples in Chapter 3
3 Language
4 Networks and Representation
5 Sociological, Psychological and other references
6 Statistical Analysis

Section 1
Work Using Network Analysis for Qualitative Data

Bliss,J. & Ogborn,J. (1977) Students' Reactions to Undergraduate
Science, Heinemann Educational Books Ltd. London
(1978) 'Les reactions des Etudiants aux situations d'apprentissage
a l'Universite'. Revue Francaise de Pedagogie Vol.45
(1979) 'The Analysis of Qualitative Data', European Journal of
Science Education, 1,5,427-440
Dumas-Carre,A. & Delacote,G. (1981) 'A Network for the Analysis of
School Exercises in Physics'. European Journal of Science
Education, 3, 4, 397-411
Griffiths,L. (1979) Talking and Understanding in Physics. Unpublished
M.Ed. Dissertation, Chelsea College, University of London
Monk,M.J. (1977) The Verbal Behaviour of Teachers and the Self-
Identity of Students in Classroom Interaction, Unpublished
M.Ed. Dissertation, Chelsea College, University of London
(1981) The Classroom Nexus: A Description of Three First Year
Classes in an Urban Comprehensive School, Together with Case
Studies of Pupils' Identities as Capable School Learners.
Unpublished Ph.D. Thesis, University of London
Mujib,F. (1980) Students' Problem Solving Behaviour in Problems
related to Undergraduate Physics with Special Attention to the
Analysis of Protocols. Unpublished Ph.D. Thesis, University of
London

Ogborn,J. (ed) (1977) Small Group Teaching in Undergraduate
Science, Heinemann Educational Books, London, (pp.92-135)
(1980) 'Some Uses of Networks of Options for Describing
Complicated Qualitative Data', in W.F. Archenhold (ed.)
Cognitive Development Research in Science and Mathematics,
University of Leeds

Section 2
References for Examples in Chapter 3

Example 1. Students' Reactions to Learning

Bliss,J. & Ogborn,J. (1977) See Section 1.
Entwistle,N.J. & Wilson,J.D. (1977) Degrees of Excellence: The
Academic Achievement Game, Hodder and Stougton, London
Flanagan,J. (1954) 'The Critical Incident Technique', Psychological
Bulletin, 51,327-358
Flood-Page,C. (1971) 'Students' Reactions to Teaching Methods',
Universities Quarterly, 25,4
Herzberg,F., Mausner,B. & Snyderman,B. (1959) The Motivation to Work
John Wiley, New York
Nisbet,J.D. & Welsh,J. (1976) 'Prediction of Failure at University,
or Failure of Prediction', British Journal of Educational
Psychology, 46,261-266
Zinberg,D.S. (1976) 'Education through Science: the Early Stages
of Career Development in Chemistry', Social Studies of Science,
6, 215-246

Example 2. Childrens' Classifications

Adlam,D.S. (1977) (with G. Turner & L. Linekar) Code in Context,
Routledge and Kegan Paul, London
Adlam,D.S. & Holland,J. (1977) Classification Strategies Employed by
Eight Year Old Children: A Study in Differences in Orientation
to Meaning, S.R.U./S.S.R.C. 5
Bernstein,B. (1971) Class, Codes and Control: Vol.1. Theoretical
Studies Towards a Sociology of Language, Routledge and Kegan
Paul, London
(1973) Class,Codes and Control: Vol.2. Applied Studies.
Towards a Sociology of Language, Routledge and Kegan Paul,
London
(1975) (revised edition 1977) Class, Codes and Control: Vol.3
Towards a Theory of Educational Transmission, Routledge and
Kegan Paul, London
Carbonnel,S. (1978) 'Classes Collectives et Classes Logiques dans la
Pensee Naturelle', Archives de Psychologie xlvi,p.177
Holland,J. (1981) 'Social Class and Changes in Orientation to
Meaning', Sociology, 15, 1,1-18

Markman,E. & Sibert,J.. (1976) 'Classes and Collections: Internal
    Organisation and Resulting Holistic Properties', Cognitive
    Psychology, 8,561-577

Example 3.   Perceptions of Pupils' Performance

Department of Education and Science (1981) A.P.U.   Science in
    Schools, Age 11 Report No.1, H.M.S.O., London
    (1982) A.P.U. Science in Schools, Age 13 Report No.1,
    H.M.S.O., London
Glass,G.V. (1977) 'Standards and Criteria'.   Paper No.10 in Occasional
    Paper Series, Evaluation Center, Western Michigan University,
    Kalamazoo
Kay,B.W. (1975) 'Monitoring Pupils' Performance', Trends in Education
    2, 11-18
    (1976) 'The Assessment of Performance Unit: Its Task and
    Rationale', Education 3-13, 4,2,108-112
Straughan,R. & Wrigley,J. (eds.) (1980) Values and Evaluation in
    Education, Harper Row, London

Example 4.   Using Networks to Represent Karen's Knowledge of Maths

Ginsburg,H. (1977) Children's Arithmetic :   The Learning Process.
    Van Nostrand, Wokingham
Hart,K.M. & Johnson,D.C. (1980) Secondary School Children's
    Understanding of Mathematics, A Report of the Mathematics
    Component of the C.S.M.S. Programme, C.S.M.E., Chelsea
    College, University of London
Shumway,R.J. (ed) (1980) Research in Mathematics Education,
    National Council of Teachers of Mathematics, Reston Virginia

Example 5.   A Network Description of Comments on Peers

Danziger,K. (1971) Socialisation, Penguin, London
Foot,H.C., Chapman,A.J. & Smith, J.R. (eds.) (1980) Friendship and
    Social Relations in Children, Wiley, New York
Hargreaves,D. (1967) Social Relations in a Secondary School,
    Routledge and Kegan Paul, London
Monk,M.J. (1981) The Classroom Nexus: A Description of Three First
    Year Classes in an Urban Comprehensive School, Together with
    Case Studies of Pupils' Identities as Capable School Learners,
    Unpublished Ph.D. Thesis, University of London
Nash,R. (1973) Classrooms Observed, Routledge and Kegan Paul,
    London

Example 6. Problem Solving by Chemistry Students

Ashmore,A.D., Frazer,M.J. & Casey,R.J. (1979) 'Problem Solving
    Networks in Chemistry', Journal of Chemical Education,
    56,6,377-379
Bree,D.S. (1975) 'Understanding of Structured Problem Solutions',
    Instructional Science, 13,327-350
Elliott,H.G. (1982) 'Links and Nodes in Problem Solving', Journal of
    Chemical Education, 59,9,719-720
Ericsson,K.A. & Simon,H.A. (1978) 'Retrospective Verbal Reports as
    Data', C.I.P. Working Paper 388, Carnegie-Mellon University
    (1979) 'Thinking-a-loud Protocols as data', C.I.P. Working
    Paper 397, Carnegie-Mellon University
Greeno,J.G. (1977) 'Process of Understanding in Problem Solving', in
    N.J. Castellan, D.B. Pisoni & G.R. Potts (eds.) Cognitive Theory
    Vol.2. John Wiley and Sons, London
Mayer,R.E. (1977) Thinking and Problem Solving: An Introduction to
    Human Cognition and Learning, Scott, Foresman and Co., Illinois
Mujib,F. (1980) See Section 1
Newell,A. & Simon,H.A. (1972) Human Problem Solving, Prentice Hall
    New Jersey
Pask,G. (1975) Conversation, Cognition and Learning, Elsevier,
    Amsterdam
Wickelgren,W.A. (1974) How to Solve Problems, W.E. Freeman and Co.
    San Francisco

Example 7. Using Networks to represent Pupils' Meanings for the Concepts of Force and Energy

Arons,A.B. (1965) Development of Concepts of Physics, Addison Wesley
    Massachusetts
Bloor,D.C, (1973) 'Are Philosophers Averse to Science?' in D.O.
    Edge and J.N. Wolpe (eds.) Meaning and Control, Tavistock,
    London
Clement,J. (1979) 'Mapping a Student's Causal Conceptions from a
    Problem Solving Protocol' in Lochhead, J. and Clement, J.
    Cognitive Process Instruction, Franklyn Institute Press,
    Philadelphia.
Coley,N.G. and Hall,V.M.D. (1980) Darwin to Einstein.   Primary
    Sources on Science and Belief, Open University/Longmans, London
Driver,R. & Easley,J. (1978) 'Pupils and Paradigms : a Review of
    the Literature Related to Concept Development in Adolescent
    Science Students', Studies in Science Education, 5, 61-84
Gilbert,J.K., Watts,D.M. & Osborne,R.J. (1982) 'Students'
    Conceptions of Ideas in Mechanics', Physics Education,
    17,2,62-66
Osborne,R.J. & Gilbert,J.K. (1979) An Approach to Student
    Understanding of Basic Concepts in Science, IET University of
    Surrey

Viennot,L. (1979) 'Spontaneous Learning in Elementary Dynamics',
European Journal of Science Education, 1,2,205-221
Watts,D.M. (1980) 'An Exploration of Students' Understanding of the
Concepts of Force and Energy', Paper Presented at the
Conference on Education for Physics Teaching, Trieste,
September 1980
Watts,D.M. (1981) 'Gravity - Don't Take it for Granted'. Physics
Education, 17,3,116-121

Example 8. Use of a Network for Item Banking

Bloom, B.S. et al. (1956) Taxonomy of Educational Objectives:
Handbook 1: Cognitive Domain, Longman, London.
Dumas-Carre,A. & Delacote,G. (1981)   See Section 1

Example 9. Language Development and the Language of Control

Halliday,M.A.K. (1975) Learning How to Mean: Explorations in the
Development of Language, Edward Arnold, London
Turner, G.J. (1973) 'Social Class and Children's Language of Control
at Age Five and Seven', in B. Bernstein (ed.) Class, Codes and
Control: Vol.2 Applied Studies Towards a Sociology of Language,
Routledge and Kegan Paul, London

Section 3
Language

Systemic Linguistics

Berry,M. (1975) An Introduction to Systemic Linguistics 1.
Structures and Systems, Batsford Books, London
(1977) An Introduction to Systemic Linguistics 2.   Levels and
Links, Batsford Books, London
Halliday,M.A.K. (1973)   Explorations in the Function of Language,
Edward Arnold, London
(1973) The Functional Basis of Language, in B. Bernstein (ed.)
Class, Codes and Control: Vol.2., Routledge and Kegan Paul,
London
(1975) Learning How to Mean: Explorations in the Development
of Language, Edward Arnold, London
Halliday,M.A.K. & Hasan,R. (1976) Cohesion in English, Longman,
London
Halliday,M.A.K. & Martin,J.R. (eds.) (1981)   Readings in Systemic
Linguistics, Batsford Books, London
Halliday,M.A.K. & Fawcett,R. (1982) New Developments in Systemic
Linguistics, Batsford Books, London

Kress,G. (ed.) (1976) Halliday: System and Function in Language, Selected Papers, Oxford University Press, London

Other Language Work

Chomsky,N. (1956) 'Three Models for the Description of Language', IRE Transactions on Information Theory, 2, 113-124
(1972) Language and Mind, Harcourt Brace, New York.
Coulthard,M. (1977) An Introduction to Discourse Analysis, Longman, London
Fillmore,C. (1968) 'The Case for Case', in E. Bach and R.T. Harms (eds.) Universals in Linguistic Theory, Holt Rinehart and Winston, New York, (pp.1-88)
Giglioli,P.P. (ed.) (1972) Language and Social Context, Penguin, London
Sinclair,J. McH. & Coulthard,R.M. (1975) Towards an Analysis of Discourse: The English Used by Teachers and Pupils, Oxford University Press, London
Turner,G.J. & Mohan,B.A. (1970) A Linguistic Description and Computer Program for Children's Speech, Routledge and Kegan Paul, London
Woods,W.A. (1975) 'What's in a Link?: Foundations for Semantic Networks', in D.G. Bobrow and A.M. Collins (eds.) Representation and Understanding, Academic Press, New York, (pp 35-82)

Section 4
Networks and representation

Aleksander,I. & Hanna,F.K., (1975) Automata Theory: An Engineering Approach. Crane Russak, New York
Boden,M. (1977) Artificial Intelligence and Natural Man, Harvester Press, Hassocks, Sussex
Busacker,R.C. & Saaty,T.L. (1965) Finite Graphs and Networks, McGraw Hill, New York
Davis,R. & King,J. (1977) 'An Overview of Production Systems' in E.W. Elcock and D. Michie (eds.) Machine Intelligence 8: Machine Representations of Knowledge, Ellis Horwood, Illinois
Findler,N.V. (ed.) (1979) Associative Networks: Representation and Use of Knowledge by Computers, Academic Press, New York
Grize,F. (1981) BARBARA: Analyse de Donnees Informelles a l'aide de Reseaux Systemiques, Ph.D. Thesis University of Neuchatel
Michie,D. (ed.) (1979) Expert Systems in the Micro-Electronic Age, Edinburgh University Press, Edinburgh
Minsky,M. (ed.) (1968) Semantic Information Processing, MIT Press Cambridge, Massachusetts
(1972) Computation: Finite and Infinite Machines, Prentice Hall, New Jersey

Minsky,M. (1974) 'A Framework for Representing Knowledge',
    Artifical Intelligence Memo 306, MIT Press Cambridge,
    Massachusetts
Quillian,R. (1968) 'Semantic Memory', in M. Minsky (ed.) Semantic
    Information Processing, MIT Cambridge, Massachusetts
Roberts,R. & Goldstein,I. (1977) 'The FRL Primer', Artificial
    Intelligence Memo 408, MIT Cambridge, Massachusetts
Schank,R.C. (1973) 'Identification of Conceptualisations Underlying
    Natural Language, in R.C. Schank and K.M. Colby (eds.)
    Computer Models of Thought and Language, W.H. Freeman, San
    Francisco
Shapiro,S.C. (1979) 'The SNePS Semantic Network Processing System',
    in N.V. Findler (ed.) Associative Networks: Representation and
    Use of Knowledge by Computers, Academic Press, New York
Winograd,T. (1972) Understanding Natural Language, Edinburgh
    University Press, Edinburgh

Section 5
Sociological, Psychological and other references

Barber,T.X. (1976) Pitfalls in Human Research: Ten Pivotal Points,
    Pergamon Press, New York
Barton,A.H. & Lazarsfeld,P.F. (1969) 'Some Functions of
    Qualitative Analysis in Social Research', in G.T. McCall
    and J.L. Simon (eds.) Issues in Participation Observation,
    Addison Wesley, New York
Blaxter,M. (ed.) (1979) 'The Analysis of Qualitative Data: a
    Symposium', The Sociological Review, 27, 4.
Blumer,H. (1954) 'What is Wrong with Social Theory?', American
    Sociological Review, 19,3-10
Bogdan,R. & Taylor,S.J. (1975) Introduction to Qualitative
    Research Methods, John Wiley, New York
Brenner,M., Marsh,P. & Brenner,M. (eds) (1978)   The Social Context
    of Method, Croom Helm, London
Bulmer,M. (ed.) (1977) Sociological Research Methods, Macmillan
    London
    (1979) 'Concepts in the Analysis of Qualitative Data'. The
    Sociological Review, 27,4,651-677
Cohen,L. & Manion,L. (1980) Research Methods in Education,
    Croom Helm, London
Douglas,M. (1973) Rules and Meanings, Penguin, London
Fransella,F. & Bannister D. (1977) A Manual for Repertory Grid
    Techniques, Academic Press, London
Halfpenny,P. (1979) 'The Analysis of Qualitative Data', The
    Sociological Review, 27,4,799-825
Hammersley,M. (1981) 'The Outsider's Advantage: a Reply to
    McNamara', British Educational Research Journal, 7, 167-171
Hudson,L. (1975) Human Beings, Jonathan Cape, London
Kelly,G.A. (1955) The Psychology of Personal Constructs, Volumes 1
    and 2 Norton, New York

Knoke,D. & Kuklinski,J.H. (1982) Network Analysis. Sage University Paper 28, Beverly Hills

Lazarsfeld,P.F. (1972) Qualitative Analysis: Historical and Critical Essays, Allyn and Bacon, Boston

Levi-Strauss,C. (1958) Anthropologie Structurale, Librairie Plon, Paris

Marsden,P.V. & Lin,N. (1982) Social Structure and Network Analysis, Sage, Beverly Hills

McCall,G.J. & Simmons,J.L. (eds.) (1969) Issues in Participant Observation, Addison Wesley, New York

McCulloch,W.S. (1965) Embodiments of Mind, M.I.T. Press, Cambridge Massachusetts

McNamara,D. (1980) 'The Outsider's Arrogance: The Failure of Pariticipant Observers to Understand Classroom Events', British Educational Research Journal, 6,113-125

Open University (1979) D.E. 304. Research Methods in Education and Social Science. Block 1. Variety in Social Science Research. Open University Press, Milton Keynes

Patton,M.Q. (1980) Qualitative Evaluation Methods, Sage, Beverly Hills, (pp295-340)

Piaget,J. (1971) Structuralism, Routledge and Kegan Paul, London (1972) The Principles of Genetic Epistemology, Routledge and Kegan Paul, London

Piatelli-Palmarini,M. (ed.) (1980) Language and Learning: The Debate between Jean Piaget and Noam Chomsky, Routledge and Kegan Paul, London

Wason,P.C. & Johnson Laird,P.N. (1977) Thinking: Readings in Cognitive Science, Cambridge University Press

Section 6
Statistical Analysis

Atkin,R.H. (1974) Mathematical Structure in Human Affairs, Heinemann, London (1981) Multidimensional Man, Penguin, London

Baker,R.J. & Nelder,J.A. (1978) GLIM Manual Release 3 NAG Library, Rothamsted Experimental Station, Harpendon, Herts, England

Bishop,Y.M.M ,Fienberg,S.E., & Holland,P.W. (1975) Discrete Multivariate Analysis, MIT Press, Cambridge, Massachusetts

Fienberg,S.E. (1978) The Analysis of Cross-Classified Data, MIT Press, Cambridge, Massachusetts

O'Muircheartaigh,C.A. & Payne,C. (1977) The Analysis of Survey Data, Vol.2, Model Fitting, John Wiley, New York

Upton,G.J.G. (1978) The Analysis of Cross-Tabulated Data, John Wiley, New York

INDEX